Keith Thayer
8-30-19

Cowboy
Poetry

Cowboy Poetry

Edited by
Julie Saffel

CASTLE BOOKS

*This here is a jack o' diamonds, a little rye whiskey, and a big helpin' of
'that's the way it is sometimes out here in the old west'—all for my Daddy.
Love You, Jule.*

This edition published by
CASTLE BOOKS ®
an imprint of Book Sales
a division of Quarto Publishing Group USA Inc.
142 West 36th Street, 4th Floor
New York, New York 10018

Designed by Tony Meisel

ISBN-13: 978-0-7858-3267-6
ISBN-10: 0-7858-3267-X

Printed in the United States of America

When the last free trail is a prim, fenced lane
    And our graves grow weeds through forgetful Mays,
Richer and statelier then you'll reign,
    Mother of men whom the world will praise.
And your sons will love you and sigh for you,
Labor and battle and die for you,
    But never the fondest will understand
    The way we have loved you, young, young land.

—from *The Plainsmen* by Charles Badger Clark, Jr.

Contents

Introduction

Before we embark on a journey through cowboy poetry, we must first familiarize ourselves with the term cowboy and gain an understanding of its meaning. What is a cowboy? According to the *Merriam-Webster's Collegiate Dictionary*, a cowboy is "one who tends cattle or horses; *especially*: a usually mounted cattle-ranch hand." This definition is very straightforward and seems a little bare-boned when compared with the idea of cowboys that we all grew up with as children. To children, and even many grown-ups, the cowboy was a romantic figure in American folklore. He was a rough and tumble loner who rode the trail on his trusty horse, cooked his meals over a campfire and slept on a bedroll beneath the stars. He always licked the badmen at the saloon and fought Indians out on the plains. With his boots, spurs, lasso and cowboy hat, he was the hero of the west. Does this sound about right? This is how the cowboy is romanticized in movies and novels and it is what every little boy wanted to be—but this isn't the real cowboy.

The term *cowboy* originated from the Spanish word *vaca* meaning *cow* and then *vaquero* meaning *cowboy*. The Spanish vaqueros were the first real cowboys, bringing cattle over from New Spain (Mexico) in the early 1500's and pushing ever northward into what we call our Southwest today. Pioneers from the United States first encountered the vaquero or cowboy on ranches around 1820, and his heyday lasted until the 1890's. The cowboy's life was a rough one, not one of romance and glamour as many imagine. He was up before dawn, in the saddle all day, spending long lonesome hours on the range, and he didn't rest until the days work was done, usually after sundown. When autumn rolled around, the cowboys rounded up the cattle, including the strays from the open range, and branded those not already branded; they kept watch over the herd during the winter months, and then in the spring, the cattle selected for market were rounded up once again and driven to the nearest railroad town, often hundreds of miles away.

The trail drive to market was a long and hard one. It usually included about 2,500 head of cattle and about a dozen cowboys to keep them all in line. When the cattle were sold, the cowboys might enjoy a short bout of carousing before returning home to start the years work once again. As for cowboy poetry and songs, they are about as old as the cowboys themselves. They originated anywhere a group of cowboys were gathered together, be it around a campfire or cookstove. They entertained one another with tall tales, humorous anecdotes and plain old good stories. These stories were passed from one cowboy to another many times over, and were oft set to rhyme or given a lively tune. Many cowboy songs also originated on the trail drives—the cowboys would sing, whistle or hum to calm down the cattle and keep themselves company on a long night. These stories and songs captured the spirit of the life led by the cowboys and the camaraderie they shared. They have been passed down through generations of cowboys and kept the fellowship alive. The poems and songs in this book are only a small portion of all that have been passed down, but they are true to form and give at least a glimmer of insight into the true cowboy way of life.

ARTHUR CHAPMAN

Out Where The West Begins

Out where the handclasp's a little stronger,
Out where the smile dwells a little longer,
    That's where the West begins;
Out where the sun is a little brighter,
Where the snows that fall are a trifle whiter,
Where the bonds of home are a wee bit tighter,
    That's where the West begins.

Out where the skies are a trifle bluer,
Out where friendship's a little truer,
    That's where the West begins;
Out where a fresher breeze is blowing,
Where there's laughter in every streamlet flowing,
Where there's more of reaping and less of sowing,
    That's where the West begins.

Out where the world is in the making,
Where fewer hearts in despair are aching,
    That's where the West begins;
Where there's more of singing and less of sighing,
Where there's more of giving and less of buying,
And a man makes friends without half trying—
    That's where the West begins.

Ridin' The Chuck-Line

I'm ridin' the chuck-line this winter;
    The bread-line they call it in town—
But it ain't so onpleasant out this way;
    Folks treat a man right when he's down;
The latchstring is out at the cabins,
    And every man makes the friend's sign;
The chuck-line ain't bad in this West-land—
    In fact I'm a-thinkin' it's fine.

I hung out a week at the Two-Bar,
    And I might' a' been stayin' there yet,
With some one to hand me the makin's
    And the light for my cigarette,
But I'd read all their novels and papers,
    And lit'rachoor's sure my best lay;
So I said 'em farewell one bright mornin'
    And I'm here with the Keystone to-day.

Oh, it's off with your saddle and bridle,
    And turn your hoss in the corral;
It's handshake and backslap and howdy,
    And draw to the fire, old pal;
Your bed is the pride of the bunkhouse,
    And you eat and you drink of the best;
There's no sort of care goin' to bother
    When you're ridin' the chuck-line out West.

The Traders

Cowboys is the durndest boys to swap;
    Two of 'em can't meet and not talk trade;
Other topics take a sudden drop
    When some crack 'bout changin' things is made.

Never seen such critters fer a deal;
    "'Lo Jim," "'Lo Bill"—I'll trade you spurs to-day";
Then they talk awhile and pass the steel
    'Fore each puncher goes his sep'rate way.

Hundred-dollar saddles changin' hands,
    Silver-mounted bridles on the go,
Hats—some havin' rattlesnakes fer bands—
    That there "swap" word never gets a "no."

Cowboys is the durndest boys to swap;
    Allus tradin' "chaps" and guns and knives;
Never seem to know just when to stop—
    Guess if they was married they'd trade wives!

The Cowboys And The Prospector

The Two-Bar camp has entertained
    A minin' feller as a guest;
He drifted in one night it rained—
    A prospector who needed rest.

He bunked with us and talked a string
    About the gold he hoped to get;
If we had let him run, by jing!
    He sure would be a-talkin' yet.

He'd scratched and dug in hills untold,
    A-huntin' fer the mother lode,
But did n't need such heaps of gold
    No more 'n the burro that he rode.

He could n't understand why we
    Was punchin' cows fer ten a week,
With not a thought that gold might be
    In every rock or hill or creek.

And we plum failed to make him out—
    His greed for what he could n't spend;
He might be right, but I misdoubt
    If such a chap could be a friend.

The Magic Mulligan

A Rider from the Two-Bar come with news from off the range:
He said he'd seen a dust cloud that looked almighty strange,
So he rode his bronco over, and there, as bold as brass,
He seen a sheepman feedin' his flock upon our grass.
The rider turned home, pronto, and he got the boys aroused,
And then they started, whoopin', for where them woollies
    browsed.
But I met 'em, on their mission, and I heard the hull bunch groan
When I said: "Now, turn back, fellers, I must play this hand alone."

I was mad clear to my gizzard when I started for the camp,
And I thought of how I'd punish this vile, sheep-herdin' scamp;
I'd escort him to the deadline, where he'd run his sheep across,
And in case I had to kill him, why, it wouldn't be much loss;
And with such thoughts churnin' in me when I spied his wagon-
    top
I rode up to the herder as he watched his woolly crop.
But he simply grinned up at me, and he said: "Now, pardner, say,
Let's set down and have some dinner 'fore we start to scrap
    to-day."

He had a stew jest ready and he dished a plateful out,
And I set and et that plateful and I heard far angels shout;
I could hear gold harps a-twangin' and my rough thoughts
    seemed to melt
As he dished another plateful and I loosened up my belt.
Then I laid aside my six-guns while the herder dished more stew,
And at last my foreman rode up, as I knowed that he would do,
And he set cross-legged with me, and he et, and more hands
    come,
And afore that sheepman's cookin' quite the loudest was struck
    dumb.

It was mulligan he'd made there, all alone out in the hills,
This here cook whose magic humbled all my fightin' Toms and
    Bills;
You kin talk of hotel dishes, made by chefs from furrin lands,
But I'll back this sheepman's cookin' 'gainst all European brands.

So I says, when we had finished: "You kin make yourself to home,
You kin pick the choicest grazin' and allow your sheep to roam;
We will drive our cattle elsewhere—you kin have whate'er you
    seek—
If you'll let us come to dinner, say about three times a week!"

The Range Pirates

Me and my hoss—that's all the firm—
    We're lords of all this Cattle Land;
The outfits writhe—but let 'em squirm—
    We're here to run our own pet brand.

We live upon the mesas high,
    And in the piñons on the plain;
They'll never catch us, though they try—
    They hunt the rustler all in vain.

We know each rock and pine-clad draw—
    We thread ten thousand cattle trails;
Then let them send the limbs of law—
    The rustler's vision never fails.

We brand the stock that others own
    And here's a gun to back each claim,
And I, who ride the plains alone,
    Have seen men shudder at my name.

So come collections, great and small—
    The world owes us a life of ease;
Me and my hoss—us two, that's all—
    We're pirates of the sagebrush seas.

The Old Dutch Oven

Some sigh for cooks of boyhood days, but none of them for me;
One roundup cook was best of all—'t was with the X–Bar–T.
And when we heard the grub-pile call at morning, noon, and
    night,
The old Dutch oven never failed to cook the things just right.

'T was covered o'er with red-hot coals, and when we fetched her
    out,
The biscuits there were of the sort no epicure would flout.
I ain't so strong for boyhood grub, 'cause, summer, spring, or fall,
The old Dutch oven baked the stuff that tasted best of all.

Perhaps 't was 'cause our appetites were always mighty sharp—
The men who ride the cattle range ain't apt to kick or carp;
But, anyway, I find myself a-dreaming of that bread
The old Dutch oven baked for us beneath those coals so red.

The Cow-Puncher's Elegy

I've ridden nigh a thousand leagues upon two bands of steel,
    And it takes a grizzled Westerner to know just how I feel;
The ranches dot the strongholds of the old-time saddle-men,
    And the glory of the cattle days can ne'er come back again.
        Oh, the creak of saddle leather—
        Oh, the sting of upland weather
When the cowmen roamed the foothills and drove in ten
    thousand steers;
        Through the years, back in the dreaming,
        I can see the camp-fires gleaming,
And the lowing of the night-herd sounds, all faintly, in my ears.

There's a checkerboard of fences, on the vast and wind swept
    range;
    And the haystacks and the windmills make the landscape new
        and strange,
And the plains are full of farmers, with their harrows and their
    ploughs;
    On the roadsides loiter kidlets, who are "driving home the
        cows!"
        Oh, the quickly faded glory
        Of the cowboy's brief, brief story!
How the old range beckons vainly in the sunshine and the rain!
        Oh, the reek of roundup battle
        And the thund'ring hoofs of cattle—
But why dream a useless day-dream, that can only give one pain?

Where have gone those trails historic, where the herders sought
    the mart?
    Where have gone the saucy cow-towns, where the gunman
        played his part?
Where has gone the Cattle Kingdom, with its armed, heroic
    strife?
    Each has vanished like a bubble that has lived its little life.
        Oh the spurs we set a-jingling,
        And the blood that went a-tingling

When we rode forth in the morning, chaps-clad knights in
    cavalcade;
        And the mem'ries that come trooping,
        And the spirits, sad and drooping,
When the cowman looks about him at the havoc Time has made.

Pete's Error

There's a new grave up on Boot Hill, where we've planted
    Rowdy Pete;
He died one evenin', sudden, with his leather on his feet;
He was Cactus Center's terror with that work of art, the Colt,
But somehow, without warnin', he up and missed his holt.

His fav'rite trick in shootin' was to grab his victim's right,
Then draw his own revolver—and the rest was jest "Good-night";
He worked it in succession on nine stout and well-armed men,
But a sickly-lookin' stranger made Pete's feet slip up at ten.

Pete had follered out his programme and had passed the fightin'
    word;
He grabbed the stranger's right hand, when a funny thing
    occurred;
The stranger was left-handed, which Pete had n't figgered out,
And, afore he fixed his error, Pete was dead beyond all doubt.

It was jest another instance of a flaw in work of man;
A lefty never figgered in the gunman's battle plan;
There ain't no scheme man thinks of that Dame Nature cannot
    beat—
So his pupils are unlearnin' that cute trick they got from Pete.

The Pony Express

The eddies swirl in the treacherous ford,
    And the clouds gather dark ahead.
And over the plain, where the sunlight poured,
    Scarce a gleam does the pale moon shed.

The pony drinks, but with gasp and sob,
    And wan is the man at its side;
The way has been long, past butte and knob,
    And still he must ride and ride.

Now the cinch is drawn and the plunge is made,
    And the bank of the stream is gained;
Eyes study the darkness, unafraid,
    And ne'er is the good horse reined.

And the hoof-beats die on the prairie vast,
    To the lone wolf's answering wail—
Thus the ghost of the Pony Express goes past
    On the grass-grown Overland Trail.

Arroyo Al On Wealth

This game of git-rich-pronto seems
    A foolish sort of thing;
The man who has such wondrous dreams
    Is wastin' time, by jing!

Which thoughts are prompted by the case
    Of Poker Bill McGuire,
Who cleaned this lively little place
    And left us broke entire.

His saddle-pockets bulged with wealth
    When Billy rode away,
But soon we found he'd won by stealth—
    Marked cards had been his lay.

And so we hit a shorter trail
    Across the foothill crags,
And nabbed that graspin', orn'ry male
    And took his saddle-bags.

And Billy's dead, his dream has bu'st
    And vanished, light as foam;
We're holdin' all his wealth in trust
    To found a orphans' home.

Arroyo Al On Worry

They'd make a rattlin' roundup, sure,
    The troubles known to man,
If we could gather all the kinds
    Since this old world began.

But 'mong the troubles on life's range,—
    The common and preferred,—
That critter labeled Worry is
    The orn'riest of the herd.

You think you've got him roped and tied
    And humbled in the dust,
But soon that critter's up again
    And raisin' clouds of dust.

You're feelin' fine—the sky is blue,
    Your laugh's a happy man's—
But Worry comes cavortin' in
    And stampedes all your plans.

Seems like, when this here world was made
    For me and you, old pal,
This Worry critter should have been
    Shut tight in some corral.

The Ostrich-Punching Of Arroyo Al

I was broke in Arizony, and was gloomy as a tomb
When I got a chance at punchin' for an outfit called Star-Plume;
I did n't ask no wherefores, but jest lit out with my tarp,
As happy as an angel with the newest make o' harp.

When I struck out for the bunkhouse, for my first day on the
    range,
I thought the tracks we follered was peculiar like and strange,
And when I asked about it, the roundup foreman sez:
"You ain't a-punchin' cattle, but are herdin' ostriches."

Well, we chased a bunch of critters on the hot and sandy plain,
Though 't was like a purp a-racin' with a U.S.A. mail train;
But at last we got 'em herded in a wire fence corral,
And the foreman sez, off-hand like: "Jest go in and rope one, Al."

Well, the first one that I tackled was an Eiffel Tower bird,
But the noose ain't pinched his thorax 'fore several things
    occurred:
He spread his millinery jest as if he meant to fly,
And then reached a stilt out, careless, and smote me above the eye.

They pulled me out from under that millin' mass o' legs,
And they fed me on hot whiskey and the yolks of ostrich eggs;
And, as soon as I was able, I pulled freight fer Cattle Land,
And the ostrich-punchin' business never gits my O.K. brand.

The Border Riders

The devil has opened his furnace door
    And poked the coals with his tail,
But we must jog on and jog some more,
    Along the outlaws' trail;
And some of us may come back again
    And some of us may not;
Plain duty's a term that is harsh to men
    In the country God forgot.

Now your throat is dry as a burned-out coal,
    And light is the old canteen,
And it's far to the nearest water-hole
    Where the slimy moisture's green;
And when you git there the spring has dried,
    You'll find, as like as not;
And that's how many a good man's died
    In the country God forgot.

But it's jog, jog on in the alkali,
    Nor let your bronco lag;
And mind the arroyos as you go by,
    Nor let your eyelids sag;
For bullets speed true in the desert land,
    Where the sand hills muffle shot,
And it's short life for him who tips his hand
    In the country God forgot.

The Cowboy And The Tempter

I met a well-dressed stranger at the bar in Poker Bill's;
I had just come off the roundup in the far Red Desert hills.
He spent his gold most lib'ral, but he overplayed his hand
When he tried to buy my cow-hoss for some distant, warrin'
    land.
He offered me two hundred, which he boosted seventy-five.
I let him talk his string out, jest to see where he'd arrive;
And he looked my pony over and then says, "I'm standin' pat
On an offer of three hundred—and you'd better grab at that!"

Well, I needed that three hundred, and I needed it plum bad,
But the thought of sellin' Teton did n't, somehow, make me glad,
And I says: "I've rode that pony in the rain and in the sun;
We have romped the range together till our thoughts melt jest like
    one;
I have trained him till in turnin' he can stand upon my hat;
You should see him on the roundup, he is quicker than a cat;
When I throw a steer, that pony holds the critter till I tie,
And he loves the game he's playin', you kin see it in his eye.

"That there hoss which you would slaughter at the front acrost
    the sea
Has shared all my daily troubles, and a comrade is to me.
We have battled snows together when King Winter's ruled the
    plains,
And we've shared the Chinook breezes and the Summer's first
    warm rains.
We have dwelt in sage and cactus till we could n't change our
    home,—
When that pony travels elsewhere, why, the rider, too, will roam.
I admit you've got me tempted, but my needs'll have to wait,
So—durn it, hoss, that stranger's up and pulled his orn'ry freight!"

The Diamond Hitch

When camp is moved, at break of day,
    Then comes old Packer Bill—a king
Who rules, with most despotic sway,
    The while he loads the pack-mule string;
"Now, stand off, fellers, give him room!
    Now, let the critter buck and pitch;
That load will stay till crack o' doom
    'Cause Bill has slung the diamond hitch."

The helpers stand in trembling awe
    And watch the ropes weave round the pack;
The artist's lightest word is law
    While strong and deft hands show their knack;
A false move condemnation brings—
    "This noose must go jest thus and sich;
No tenderfoot must bobble things
    When Old Bill slings the diamond hitch."

Old Bill is gone—and o'er the ways
    His caravans trailed, in the past,
The engine thunders through the haze
    That hangs above the prairie vast;
But ere the dawn of life is fanned,
    Disclosing land of fence and ditch,
I seem to seek the pack-mules stand
    While old Bill slings the diamond hitch.

The Bunkhouse

The bunkhouse on the cattle ranch
    Was lowly, but at night
When its small window was aglow
    We hurried to that light,
And merrily we trooped within
    And flung our saddles down,
And there were tales for all to hear
    Told by the plainsmen brown.

The bunkhouse walls were papered o'er
    With scraps from everywhere—
With pictures of great battleships
    And ladies who were fair;
And all could read strange bits of news,
    While many comrades' scrawls
Were written there, illegibly,
    Upon the bunkhouse walls.

I've traveled many miles since then,
    But oft, when sets the sun,
I think about the bunkhouse, low,
    Where cowboys, one by one,
Came strolling in to chat and smoke
    And play a game of cards;
I'd even stand for their long snores—
    Where are you, good old pards!

The Market Train

The old caboose is rattlin', and is swayin' to and fro;
    But we 're fog-bound in tobacco, while the tales like magic
        grow;
There's a big trainload of cattle that is shriekin' down the grades,
    But we're settin' back contented while we hear of feuds and
        raids;
There's Ed and Bill and Curly, and a man from Pecos way—
    We're the chaperons of shipments that are fresh from prairie
        hay;
His load of care is lifted and he feels like givin' cheers
    When the cowman goes to market with the season's first
        prime steers.

The stories last till midnight, while the old train onward roars;
    There are tales of blood and slaughter and of evenin'-up old
        scores;
There are stories of the prairie and stories of the hills,
    And of deeds of heroism with the mildest full of thrills.
The smoke keeps gettin' thicker, but nobody wants to quit—
    There's another story comin', and it's sure to make a hit;
There's history for the writin'—old Homer'd be all ears
    And could write another winner on a trainload of beef steers.

Tex

Tex was all we called him, in them days—
    Tex was all the name he answered to;
"Tex," we hollered 'cross the prairie ways
    When we called him to his beans and stew;
Tex was all he told us when he come,
    Tex was all be told us when he went;
Tex was all he needed, too, by gum!
    Nothin' else would fit him worth a cent.

Tex was long and lean, and Tex was brown,
    Tex was sure a wizard with the rope,
Tex could drink and stir up things in town—
    Allus hit the high spots on a lope;
Tex could gamble—likewise Tex could shoot
    Quicker than a streak of lightnin' bright,
Tex could shake his shapely, high-heeled boot
    In a dance and never quit all night.

Tex was sure a hit around the place;
    Tex was allus leadin' work and play;
No one looked for Tex to hunt disgrace
    When be said good-bye to us one day;
But he's gone and done it, sure enough—
    Tex is past all hope, so men relate;
Tex is now—gee whiz! but it seems tough—
    Gov'nor of some doggone Eastern State!

The Old-Timer

He showed up in the springtime, when the geese began to honk;
He signed up with the outfit, and we fattened up his bronk;
His chaps were old and tattered, but he never seemed to mind,
'Cause fer worryin' and frettin' he had never been designed;
He's the type of cattle-puncher that has vanished now, of course,
With his hundred-dollar saddle on his twenty-dollar horse.

He never seemed to bother over fortune's ups and downs,
And he never quit his singin' when the gang was full of frowns;
He would lose his roundup money in an hour of swift play,
But he never seemed discouraged when he ambled on his way.
He would hit the trail a-singin', and his smile was out full force,
Though he'd lost his fancy saddle and he did n't have a horse.

I have wondered where he wanders in these late, degenerate years,
When there are no boundless ranges, and there are no long-horn
    steers;
But I'll warrant he is cheerful, though unfriendly is the trail,
And his cigarette is glowing, though his grub supply may fail,
For he had life's happy secret—he had traced it to the source
In his hundred-dollar saddle on his twenty-dollar horse.

Men In The Rough

Men in the rough—on the trails all new-broken—
    Those are the friends we remember with tears;
Few are the words that such comrades have spoken—
    Deeds are their tributes that last through the years.

Men in the rough— sons of prairie and mountain—
    Children of nature, warm-hearted, clear-eyed;
Friendship with them is a never-sealed fountain;
    Strangers are they to the altars of pride.

Men in the rough—curt of speech to their fellows—
    Ready in everything, save to deceive;
Theirs are the friendships that time only mellows,
    And death cannot sever the bonds that they weave.

ROBERT V. CARR

When Dutchy Plays The Mouth Harp

When Dutchy plays the mouth harp, ev'ry
    puncher gathers 'round
To help on with the music by a-stompin'
    on the ground;
An' the cook he throws a shuffle an' the night
    hawk pats his hand,
When Dutchy plays the mouth harp in a
    way to beat the band:
  Oh, my girl she has a turned-up nose,
  A turned-up nose, a turned-up nose,
  Wella, wella, wella, I suppose
  That she can't help that turned-up nose.

When Dutchy plays the mouth harp an' we've
    cached our chuck away,
An' ev'ryone a-havin' fun an' feelin' mighty gay,
There's nothin' we likes better than to lend a
    helpin' hand,
When Dutchy plays the mouth harp in a way
    to beat the band:
  Oh, my girl has got a pinto face,
  A pinto face, a pinto face,
  Wella, wella, wella, who did place
  Them freckles on her little face?

When Dutchy plays the mouth harp—does
    a cake walk something fine—
'Tis then us old cowpunchers come a-siftin'
    down the line
A-swingin' an' a-shuf-fel'in' an' pattin' o' the
    hand,
When Dutchy plays the mouth harp in a way
    to beat the band:
  Oh, my girl she wears a number nine,
  A number nine, a number nine,
  Wella, wella, wella, it's a sign,
  She might as well be wearin' mine.

The Bronco Buster

You rough-necks think it plenty fun
To set up there an' josh an' run
Your talk-machines an' watch me take
This here old coffin-head to break.

"Stay with him, fan him!" What you say?
"Pull leather?" Nix; I'm here to stay;
No bronk that ever lived or growed,
This prairie chicken ever throwed.

(It hain't because I hate this hoss,
It's jes' because I will be boss;
I'll make him know an' not ferget,
That I am allers boss, you bet!)

See that! he's gentlin' down an' he
Tomorrow will jes' foller me
An' let me scratch his head an' cheek,
A lamb he'll beat fer bein' meek.

Oh, laff, you gobblers, have your fun,
But when with this here job I'm done,
I'll show you would-be's this bronk change,
An' lead the best hoss on the range.

Prairie Wolves

Up where the white bluffs fringe the plain,
When heaven's lights are on the wane,
They sing their songs as demons might
Shriek wild a chorus to the night.
Gaunt, gray brutes with dripping fangs,
And eyes aflame with hunger-pangs,
With lips curled back in snarls of hate,
They wail a curse against their fate.

An Oracle Of The Plains

A bow-legged cowboy sat rolling, one day,
A cute cigarette in his own nimble way;
And when he had finished the coffin nail, he
Delivered this wisdom free gratis to me:

"What's the use fer to worry, or even to fret,
Fer the things of the world you never will get?
An' likewise she's true that fer me or fer you,
There's jes' about one or two tricks we can do;
Be as good as we know an' cut out the bad,
An' alters be cheerful an' never get mad;
Fer the frownin' face gathers the wrinkles,
    my friend,
An' the smilin' one stays like a boy's to the
    end."

Thus, the bow-legged puncher delivered advice
In a style not offensive but studiously nice;
And then smiling quaintly he winked at the sky
In a way that was childish but wickedly sly.

The Chuck Wagon

Cowpuncher's cafay,
It is that-o-way,
An' we strike it kerslam 'bout three times
    a day;
When cook yells, "Come get it!"
He don't have to plead,
"Hi yip! all you logies, come gather your feed!"

Cowboy's Salvation Song

Oh, it's move along, you dogies, don't be
    driftin' by the way,
Fer there's goin' to be a roundup an' a-cut-
    tin' out, they say,
Of all the devil's rangers an' a-movin' at sun-
    rise,
An' you'd better be preparin' fer a long drive
    to the skies.

Oh, it's move along, you dogies, don't be driftin' by the
    way,
Fer the boss of all the rus'lers is a-comin'
    'round today;
So you better be a-movin', throw your dust
    right in his eyes,
An' hit the trail a-flyin' fer the home ranch in the skies.

So it's move along, you dogies, fer the devil
    has in hand
A bunch of red-hot irons an' he's surely goin'
    to brand
All his cattle an' some others, an' mighty
    sudden, too,
So you'd better be a-movin' so he won't be
    brandin' you.

Oh, it's move along, you dogies, tho' you have
    the mange o' sin,
There's a range you're sure to shake it when
    you come a-trailin' in,
Where the grass is allers growin' an' the
    water's allers pure,
So it's sift along, you dogies, 'fore the devil
    brands you sure.

Spring

Spring is here,
And the brand-new calf
Doth wobble 'round with mellow
Laugh.
The chickens cluck,
And the glad, young bronco
Snorting there,
In all his mad delight doth try
To kick the
Scroll work
Off
The
Sky.

Dance, You Punchers, Dance

Oh, whoop it up an' let's be gay,
It's a long time now 'til break o' day;
So fer a good time get a hunch,
An' cut your girl from out the bunch—
    An' say—
        You may
  Start them fiddles right away,
    An' Jiggin' Finn
        With his 'cor'din
  Will do the rest, so all join in,
An' pound the floor with your high-heeled
    boot,
An' swing your granger girl so cute,
  An' dance, you punchers, dance.

Oh, lips are sweet an' eyes are bright,
'Tis sparkin' time fer all tonight;
So lope along an' do your best,
An' cut right in an' lead the rest.
    An' say—
        You may
  Start them fiddles right away,
    An' Jiggin' Finn
        With his 'cor'din
  Will do the rest, so all join in,
An' pound the floor with your high-heeled
    boot,
An' swing your granger girl so cute,
  An' dance, you punchers, dance.

There's drink an' fodder fer you-all,
My land-o'-goodness! hear that call!
The set's a-formin'! Cut loose now!
An' show them bashful fellers how—
    An' say—
        You may
  Start them fiddles right away,
    An' Jiggin' Finn

With his 'cor'din
Will do the rest, so all join in,
An' pound the floor with your high-heeled
boot,
An' swing your granger girl so cute,
An' dance, you punchers, dance.

A Light Joke

Tho' in a bunk house on a ranch,
    No 'lectric lights are present,
We slaps a candle in a can,
    An' calls it in-can-des'ent.
An' if you jes' must know the rest,
    You might as well look pleasant,
An' laff like blazes when we names
    Our light a tin-can-des'ent.

An' A Two-Step's What They Play

A little queen in calico,
    Her smiles—them killin' smiles—
Be jes' some o' a thousand
    Of her wicked ways an' wiles;
An' she's the smoothest dancer
    Most anywhere you'll see,
An' you ought to see her two-step,
    La-de-da, along with me.

Oh, she's light as any feather,
    The music's simply fine,
An' I jes get plum' loco
    When her face is close to mine.
Fer my heart is thinkin' something
    My lips don't dast to say,
When she leans agin my shoulder
    An' a two-step's what they play.

I could dance with her ferever,
    Wisht we never'd get thro',
'Cause Time jes' takes a lay-off,
    An' reason quits work, too.
Seems ev'rything has ended,
    Fer a spell fergot to be,
When they plays a two-step sweetly
    An' she drifts away with me.

The Spring Roundup

A world of dust peopled by strange shapes
    That whirl and plunge and rear,
A carnival of sound, deep, wild and hoarse,
    That speaks maternal fear.
Stern work for man and trusty horse,
    Swing out, swing in and pass!
The day is hot and long, but yet
    Tonight, upon the grass,
The horse will ease his fevered sides
    And man will count it blest
To smoke and talk and lastly know
    The pleasant range of rest.

The Camp's Asleep

The camp's asleep and thro' the gloom,
The white-topped wagons spectral loom;
And weird the lonesome coyotes call,
And quiet stars stand watch o'er all.
The fire's down, the shadows creep,
Their work is done, the camp's asleep.

The Tryst

I've ridden since the day throwed back
    The trailers of the night,
An' what fer, shall I tell you,
    In a stampede o' delight?
To wait out by the cottonwoods,
    An' dove-call softly to
A girl I know will answer:
    "I'm a-comin', boy, to you."

'Twas no time to spare my bronco;
    His breathin' spells were brief;
He's white with foam an' shakin'
    Like the Chinook shakes the leaf.
Fer I've splashed thro' muddy rivers,
    An' loped across divides,
An' ridden where no puncher
    In his reason ever rides.

Thro' wallers caked with gumbo,
    The buffalo once knew;
Thro' water holes an' washouts,
    An' a-boggin' in the slew.
O'er alkali an' sage brush flats
    I cut the whistlin' breeze,
An' come straight as the eagle
    When his lady bird's to please.

I'm a-watchin' an' I'm waitin'
    With heart as light as air,
As happy as they make 'em,
    Either here or anywhere.
Jes' to listen fer her footfall,
    An' hear her sweet voice thro'
The prairie silence murmur,
    "I'm a-comin', boy, to you."

Sage Brush

A dusty trail, a burning sky,
And splotch of leprous alkali;
Gray, somber wastes that touch the rim
Of Shadow Land, vast, vague and dim.

Fer I'm A Boy

Where is th' best huntin' now?
  Where do th' rabbits go
An' make their tracks an' leave their trails
  Across th' nice new snow?
      I guess I know—
      I guess I know,
        Fer I'm a boy.

Where has th' squirrel his cupboard an'
  Th' little chipmonk, too?
An' lots an' lots of secrits that
  I hain't a-tellin' you—
      I guess I know—
      I guess I know,
        Fer I'm a boy.

Where is th' chickens gone an' hid—
  Th' ones what whirs their wings?
Why, you don't know much as a kid,
  About such common things—
      I guess I know—
      I guess I know,
        Fer I'm a boy.

That There Girl

It's that there girl 'most all the time,
Fer workin' I hain't worth a dime;
An' jes' can't turn around or stir
Without some foolish thought o' her.
Can scarcely sleep or eat my chuck—
Dog-gone the luck! I guess I'm stuck!

The Night Stampede

The thunder rolled like a thousand drums,
    And the sky was torn in twain
With a livid wound, and then the hiss
    Of the madly lashing rain.

The herd swept on down the trail of doom,
    As a flare of yellow light
For a heart-beat shone on him who rode
    By the side of Death that night.

Oh, the clashing horns and grinding hooves,
    And the flick of pistol flame,
And he who headed that wild stampede,
    Lone hero without a name!

Oh, the awful rush of plunging shapes,
    When the last, last stumble came,
And the crash to earth of horse and man—
    Death won, aye, he won the game.

The Winds Of The West

Oh, the west winds, the wild winds, glad vagrants and free,
They sing of the lure of the long trail to me;
They sing of a bluff, a lone wolf on the crest,
And the tang of the sage from the wastes to the west.

Oh, the west winds, the wild winds, a mad symphony
That shouts of the smoke of the line camps to me;
And out of my soul bursts a passionate cry,
"Oh, I come, I come home, for thy bondman am I."

The End Of The Trail

'Tween the old time and the new,
I have sung heart-songs of you—
You, lean stranger to all fear,
Careless border cavalier.

Now, old pard, that you are gone,
And the gray and cheerless dawn
Of a day called Progress comes,
And the throaty engine hums
Down the trail where you and I
Made our camps and watched the sky
Drop it's crimson sunset bars
To a bunch of mav'rick stars—
Then, oh, then, I cry aloud
Curses on the white-faced crowd,
On the heights of stone and wood,
Standing where our line camps stood;
On the jangle of the street,
And each pale worn face I meet.

On the coyote ways of men—
Sharp of fang beyond our ken—
Snapping o'er a brother's bones
For a pile of yellow stones.
Did we seek for gold or fame?
No, we played a careless game;
And on plunging ponies we
Shouted back in mocking glee,
When in town the black gun spoke
Thro' a smiling wreath of smoke.

Thus I dream and long and fret,
For my heart will not forget—
Not forget those old, red days
Of the trail—its careless ways;
Not forget—you know the sign—
Answer me, oh, pard of mine.

WILLIAM LAWRENCE CHITTENDEN

The Cowboy's Christmas Ball

To the Ranchmen of Texas

'Way out in Western Texas, where the Clear Fork's waters flow,
Where the cattle are "a-browzin'," an' the Spanish ponies grow;
Where the Northers "come a-whistlin'" from beyond the Neutral
    strip;
And the prairie dogs are sneezin' as if they had "The Grip";
Where the cayotes come a-howlin' 'round the ranches after dark,
And the mocking-birds are singin' to the lovely "medder lark";
Where the 'possum and the badger, and rattlesnakes abound,
And the monstrous stars are winkin' o'er a wilderness profound;
Where lonesome, tawny prairies melt into airy streams,
While the Double Mountains slumber, in heavenly kinds of
    dreams;
Where the antelope is grazin' and the lonely plovers call—
It was there that I attended "The Cowboys' Christmas Ball."

The town was Anson City, old Jones's county seat,
Where they raise Polled Angus cattle, and waving whiskered
    wheat;
Where the air is soft and "bammy," an' dry an' full of health,
And the prairies is explodin' with agricultural wealth;
Where they print the *Texas Western,* that Hec. McCann supplies,
With news and yarns and stories, uv most amazin' size;
Where Frank Smith "pulls the badger," on knowin' tenderfeet,
And Democracy's triumphant, and mighty hard to beat;
Where lives that good old hunter, John Milsap from Lamar,
Who used to be the Sheriff, back East, in Paris, sah!"
'T was there, I say, at Anson, with the lively "widder Wall,"
That I went to that reception, "The Cowboys' Christmas Ball."

The boys had left the ranches and come to town in piles;
The ladies— "kinder scatterin'"— had gathered in for miles.
And yet the place was crowded, as I remember well,
'T was got for the occasion, at "The Morning Star Hotel."
The music was a fiddle an' a lively tambourine,
And a "viol come imported," by the stage from Abilene.

The room was togged out gorgeous—with mistletoe and shawls,
And candles flickered frescoes, around the airy walls.
The "wimmin folks" looked lovely—the boys looked kinder
treed,
Till their leader commenced yellin': "Whoa! fellers, let's
stampede,"
And the music started sighin', an' awailin' through the hall,
As a kind of introduction to "The Cowboys' Christmas Ball."

The leader was a feller that came from Swenson's Ranch,
They called him "Windy Billy," from "little Deadman's Branch."
His rig was "kinder keerless," big spurs and high-heeled boots;
He had the reputation that comes when "fellers shoots."
His voice was like a bugle upon the mountain's height;
His feet were animated, an' a *mighty, movin' sight,*
When he commenced to holler, "Neow fellers, stake yer pen!
"Lock horns ter all them heifers, an' russle 'em like men.
"Saloot yer lovely critters; neow swing an' let 'em go,
"Climb the grape vine 'round 'em—all hands do-ce-do!
"You Mavericks, jine the round-up—Jest skip her waterfall,"
Huh! hit wuz gettin' active, "The Cowboys' Christmas Ball!"

The boys were tolerable skittish, the ladies powerful neat,
That old bass viol's music *just got there with both feet!*
That wailin', frisky fiddle, I never shall forget;
And Windy kept a singin'—I think I hear him yet—
"O Xes, chase your squirrels, an' cut 'em to one side,
"Spur Treadwell to the centre, with Cross P Charley's bride,
"Doc. Hollis down the middle, an' twine the ladies' chain,
"Varn Andrews pen the fillies in big T Diamond's train.
"All pull yer freight tergether, neow swallow fork an' change,
"'Big Boston' lead the trail herd, through little Pitchfork's range.
"Purr 'round yer gentle pussies, neow rope 'em! Balance all!"
Huh ! hit wuz gettin' active—"The Cowboys' Christmas Ball!"

The dust riz fast an' furious, we all just galloped 'round,
Till the scenery got so giddy, that Z Bar Dick was downed.
We buckled to our partners, an' told 'em to hold on,
Then shook our hoofs like lightning, until the early dawn.
Don't tell me 'bout cotillions, or germans. No sir 'ee!
That whirl at Anson City just takes the cake with me.

I'm sick of lazy shufflin's, of them I've had my fill,
Give me a frontier break-down, backed up by Windy Bill.

McAllister ain't nowhar! When Windy leads the show,
I've seen 'em both in harness, and so I sorter know—
Oh, Bill, I sha'n't forget yer, and I'll oftentimes recall,
That lively gaited sworray—"The Cowboy's Christmas Ball."

The Round-Up

With the joy of the wind in our hearts and our faces,
    We drive the shy cattle across the divide;
Hurrah for the zest and the swift reckless races
    That make up the pleasures of such a wild ride!

Through mesquite and cactus and *chapparral* bushes,
    Over oceans of blossoms we gallop along;
On, on! toward the round-up our stout broncho rushes,
    As we drive up the stragglers with shout and with song.

We have searched the lone canyon and scoured-the valley;
    We are driving the mavericks, the calves and the steers;
On, on, toward the outfit, where stockmen all rally,
    To claim hoofed possessions by brands and marked ears.

Oh, the roaring and surging and pawing of cattle!
    How they bellow and stampede and long to be free!
How their lowered heads crash as they lock horns in battle!
    How their billowed backs heave like some wild tawny sea!

While cowboys and "nesters" stand guard on swift horses,
    The range boss's outfit rides in through the herd
Cutting out and inspecting—grim, trained, active forces
    That divide up the cattle without a waste word.

Each man "holds" his own, then the roping and branding;
    Ye gods, this is sport! see that yearling career;
The lasso has caught him! See that bowed broncho standing
    As firm as a rock, with his head to the steer.

When the day's work is over to "camp" we are flying,
    To unsaddle and hobble and joke with the cook;
When the supper is finished, there's a *round-up of lying*,
    But the tales that we tell are not told in this book.

Texas Types—The Cowboy

He wears a big hat and big spurs and all that,
    And leggins of fancy fringed leather;
He takes pride in his boots and the pistol he shoots,
    And he's happy in all kinds of weather.

He is fond of his horse—'t is a bronco, of course,
    For, oh, he can ride like the Devil;
He is old for his years, and he always appears
    To be foremost at round-up or revel.

He can sing, he can cook, yet his eyes have the look
    Of a man that to fear is a stranger;
Yes, his cool, quiet nerve will always subserve
    In his wild life of duty and danger.

He gets little to eat and he guys tenderfeet,
    And for Fashion—oh, well, he's "not in it!"
He can rope a gay steer when he gets on his ear;
    At the rate of two-forty a minute!

His saddle's the best in the wild, woolly West,
    Sometimes it will cost sixty dollars;
Ah, he knows all the tricks, when he brands
    "Mavericks,"
    But his learning's not gained from your scholars.

He is loyal as steel, but demands a square deal,
    And he hates and despises a coward.
Yet the cowboy you'll find unto woman is kind,
    Though he'll fight till by death overpowered.

Hence I say unto you, give the cowboy his due,
    And be kinder, my friends, toward his folly;
For he's generous and brave, though he may not behave
    Like your dudes, who are so melancholy.

Texas Types—The Sheriff

He's a quiet, easy fellow, with his pants tucked in his boots,
And he wears a big revolver which he seldom ever shoots;
He has served his time as ranger on the reckless Rio Grande,
And he has the reputation for great marksmanship and sand;
He has strung up several horse thieves in the rustler days gone by,
And although he seems so pleasant there's a devil in his eye.

When he goes to take a prisoner, he calls him by his name,
In that confidential manner which suggests the bunco game;
If the culprit is not willing, takes exception to the plan,
Our Sheriff gets the drop, sir, and he likewise gets his man;
Oh, it's "powerful persuadin'," is a pistol 'neath your nose,
"Hands up, you've got to go, Sam," and Sam he ups and goes.

In the fall at "County 'lections" when the candidates appear,
The Sheriff's awful friendly, for he loves to "'lectioneer";
Then he takes the honest granger and ye stockman by the hand,
And he *augers* them for votes, sir, in a manner smooth and bland;
He is generous, brave, and courtly, but a dangerous man to sass,
For his manner is suggestive of that sign—"*Keep off the grass!*"

He may run a livery stable, or perchance he keeps hotel;
He may own a bunch of cattle, or may have some lots to sell;
He is full of *go* and travel, for he's paid so much per mile,
And his little bills for "extras," make County judges smile.
"Hyars lookin' at yer," Sheriff; come, boys, lets drink her down,
To the most important man, sir! of every Texas town.

Texas Types—The Cattle Queen

In the lovely land of Texas,
Where the "rustlers" seldom vex us,
And the "Legislature checks us
    With its land laws if you please"—
There, within a hacienda,
Dwells a lady dark and slender,
Who is radiant, rare, and tender—
    The dashing little widow—Mistress Breeze.

She is pretty as a fairy,
She is gay, and glad, and airy,
Is that queen of the "perairie,"
    She's the dearest of our joys,
You'll surrender when you meet her,
When you see this fair chiquita;
Yes, you'll love this señorita,
    It's the fate of all the boys.

She is graceful as a lily,
But she knocks the stockmen silly
When she rides her lively filly
    Round the ranges after steers.
She can rope a maverick yearling
With her light riatta twirling;
Oh, I oft have seen it curling
    'Round some bawling brindle's ears.

She owns thirty thousand cattle,
And a bank up in Seattle;
Oh, she makes the dollars rattle
    When she goes to San Antone—
Oh, I tell you she's a winner,
Who can cook and grace a dinner
For a famished bachelor sinner,
    That will make his spirit groan.

Yes, she "raises the old Harry"
With the boys—and *likewise Larry,*—
But, alas, she will not marry,
    She's so *"powerful hard to please,"*
Yet mankind is still her debtor,
For she makes her wild world better,
And I thank God that I met her,—
    This lovely little widow—Mistress Breeze.

Texas Types—The Tenderfoot

You can tell him by his "weepons!"
    And his soft, confiding air,
His bran-new gorgeous outfit,
    And his high-priced aged mare.

He is primed with tales of dangers
    In the wild and woolly West,
And bold dreams of robber rangers
    Disturb his nightly rest.

He has queer ideas of Texas;
    Thinks her people live in gore!
He seems queer to all the sexes,
    For his actions make folks roar.

But he soon gets used to chaff, sir,
    For he's green as April wheat,
Yet for men to make you laugh, sir,
    I commend the Tenderfeet.

Soon he pines to be a cowboy
    And to ride a pitching horse,
Ah, then you ought to see him.
    For he's paralyzed—of course.

Then he writes some lying story
    To his family far away,
Some brave tale of border glory
    Where he figures in the play.

If he goes back where he came from,
    He assumes a Western air,
Then I tell you he is woolly!
    And his actions make folks stare.

Yes, you know I tell the truth, Sir,
    Now I never lie for pelf,
But I was—yes! in my youth, sir,
    Was a Tenderfoot myself!!

The Ranchman's Ride

Hurrah for a ride on the prairies free,
   On a fiery untamed steed,
Where the curlews fly and the cayotes cry,
And the fragrant breeze goes whispering by;
   Hurrah! and away with speed.

With left hand light on the bridle-rein,
   And saddle-girths cinched behind,
With lariat tied at the pommel's side,
And lusty bronchos true and tried,
   We'll race with the whistling wind.

We are off and away, like a flash of light
   As swift as the shooting star,
As an arrow flies towards its distant prize,
On! on we whirl toward the shimmering skies;
   Hurrah! hurrah! hurrah!

As free as a bird o'er billowy sea
   We skim the flowered Divide,
Like seamews strong we fly along,
While the earth resounds with galloping song
   As we plunge through the fragrant tide.

Avaunt with your rides in crowded towns!
   Give me the prairies free,
Where the curlews fly and the cayotes cry,
And the heart expands 'neath the azure sky;
   Ah! that's the ride for me.

A San Antonio Memory

In old San Antonio city,
    Where the soldiers' bugles blow,
Dwelt a lady proud and stately,
    Years and years and years ago.
Dark was she, this Senorita,
    Lovely as some queen of Spain,
And her voice was soft, and sweeter
    Than the songs of summer rain.

There she lived beside a river,
    Where the winding waters flow
On and on and on forever,
    To the Gulf of Mexico.
There in dreams of Spanish splendor,
    Midst a grove of stately trees,
Stood her gray old hacienda,
    Home of birds and flowers and bees.

Ah, that dear, old-fashioned garden
    With its wealth of rare perfume,
Seemed of old a glimpse of Eden,
    Lost in tangled bowers of bloom.
There the night-winds sobbed their stories
    Round some lonely little mounds;
There the mosses' drooping glories
    Draped a family's burying-grounds.

There of old we often pondered,
    Listening to the waters flow;
There of old we talked and wandered,
    Years and years and years ago.
Oft when twilight's kiss was stealing
    O'er the skies in golden beams,
And the mission bells were pealing
    Vesper songs of poet's dreams,

We would seek some seat embowered
    'Neath the old magnolia trees,
Where the zephyrs' kisses showered
    Rarest fragrance to the breeze.
There we dreamed beside that river
    There we heard the bugles trill,
Till the echoes seemed to quiver
    Through the evening calm and still.

Then my lady of the villa
    Soft would strum her light guitar,
To some tune of old Sivella,
    Or some song from Alcazar.
Ah, those old extravaganzas,
    How they soothed my restless heart;
Ah, those dreamy, sad romanzas
    From my life will ne'er depart.

But to-night I'm sad and weary,
    Listening to the Northers blow,
For the wind is wild and dreary,
    And I dream of long ago.
Gone is now that hacienda,
    Gone that garden known of yore;
Hushed alas that voice so tender—
    Hushed, and lost forever more.

The Country To The West

When the hull big world gits gloomy and as dark as all tarnation,
    And a feller feels as grumpy as a lone steer on the range;
When he cain't see nothin' 'round him but despair and desolation,
    'Cuz the trails that he is follerin' are new and fresh and
        strange;
When the people that he's meetin' ain't the kind he likes to chum
    with,
    And he feels a homesick feelin' jest a-tuggin' 'neath his vest,
How he hankers for the open, and the pals he used to bum with
    In the sagebrush stretches lyin' in the country to the West!

And he glimpses wide arroyos stretchin' out as if to greet him,
    While the rocky buttes they lure him, and they whisper to
        him, "Come!"
And the hoary mountains call him, and the cattle trails entreat
    him
    To forget the busy city and its life so burdensome.
There's a whisper from the mesas which forever haunts his
    dreamin',
    And his heart rebels within him with its burden of unrest,
And he sees the sand-dunes sparklin' and the yucca-plumes a-
    gleamin'
    In the sagebrush stretches lyin' in the country to the West!

There's the croonin' of the pine trees—jest forever callin',
    There's the murmur of the river as it glides through chasms
        deep;
There's the lowin' of the cattle on his restless senses fallin',
    And the yelpin' of the ki-yote, as he's droppin' off to sleep.
There's the purpled sunsets sparklin' like a molten sea off yonder,
    There's a glint of gold a-shinin' on the rugged canyon's crest,
And the vision stands before him, growin' dearer, growin' fonder
    Of the sagebrush stretches lyin' in the country to the West.

Oh, there ain't no spot that's dearer in the hull of God's creation,
    When you've felt the call within you, as you packed your kit
        to go!
And you had a mental picture of the lonely railroad station
    Where the boys would ride to meet you—all the pals you
        used to know.
How the rangelands smiled upon you, and the skies seemed all the
    bluer,
    With the prairie jest a-blazin' with the blooms upon its breast!
Then you knew that life was sweeter, and your pards were kinder,
    truer,
    In the sagebrush stretches lyin' in the country to the West.

The Old Bunkhouse

'Tis empty and silent, all sagging and creaking,
　　With windows agape to the breezes that blow;
The rafters are cobwebbed, the hinges are squeaking,
　　As idly the winds swing the door to and fro.
The dust and the mold have left visible traces,
　　The hearthstone is cold, and 'tis cheerless and strange,
And vainly I look for the bronzed, fearless faces
　　Of riders I bunked with out there on the range.

I listen for voices of old pals to greet me,
　　But out from the shadows no echoes I hear;
No rough, hearty handclasp of pardners to meet me,
　　No laughter or singing falls sweet on my ear.
The pack-rats go scampering boldly around there,
　　And squeak their defiance about the dim room,
Naught else, only grim desolation, is found there,
　　The place is abandoned to silence and gloom!

The empty corrals have no dust-clouds arising
　　Where restless cowponies are milling inside;
No loud-swearing puncher is vainly devising
　　A means of subduing a range outlaw's pride.
The long, straggling columns of cattle have vanished,
　　The draws and the coulees are empty and lone;
The plow and the reaper the brand-iron have banished—
　　No more is the saddle the Westerner's throne!

'Tis only a relic of song and of story—
　　The bunkhouse that stands in the shine and the rain.
A silent reminder of cattle-day glory
　　That leaves me a feeling of sadness and pain.
But often I think, in my fireside dreaming,
　　Of days when the cowman was monarch and king,
And picture, in fancy, the bunkhouse lights gleaming,
　　And echo the trail-songs the cowboys would sing!

The Stampede

A lowering night, with muggy, sultry air;
    A thirsting, restless, sullen, bawling herd;
Low distant rumbling peals of thunder there;
    A sky with vivid lightning-flashes blurred.
The flickering campfire's dull and feeble glow;
    The ribald songs the grim night-herders sing;
The murmur of the river, faint and low;
    The night-bird overhead, on tireless wing.

From rugged buttes, in snarling monotone,
    The muttering thunder speaks a warning grim;
The breeze which o'er the rolling height is blown,
    Sighs fitfully across the mesa's brim.
Now vagrant rain-drops kiss the dusty ground,
    As louder growls the thunder notes on high;
The cattle low in terror at the sound,
    While anxious riders watch the threatening sky.

And now the storm bursts forth in fury wild,
    And jagged lightning flashes leap and flare
Across the heavens, where inky clouds are piled,
    While crash on crash re-echoes through the air!
In mad affright the herd is under way!
    No hand their headlong rushes can restrain!
And blinding, glaring shafts of light display
    A sea of clashing horns across the plain!

Into the pitchy darkness of the night,
    With spur and quirt and shot and wild hello,
Lithe figures speed to check their frenzied flight,
    As on the panic-stricken thousands go!

• • • • •

And now the Storm God's wrath is spent and gone;
    Hushed is his voice upon the mesa's crest;
The stars peep forth through scudding clouds, and
    dawn
    Finds wearied riders safe; the herd at rest.

The Trail-Herd

Clouded sun an' coolin' morn;
    Squeakin' "taps" an' spurs a-rattle;
Loungin' 'crost my saddlehorn
    Trailin' dull-eyed, bawlin' cattle.
Chokin' dust-clouds in the air,
    Off across the range a-driftin';
Punchers cussin' stragglers there
    As the mornin' mist is liftin'.

Wild-eyed mavericks on the prod;
    Plungin' ponies, buckin', snortin',
Or across the sun-baked sod,
    Full o' ginger a-cavortin'.
Ol' chuckwagon on ahead,
    Gittin' of the grub-pile ready;
Sun a-blazin' fiery red;
    Calves a-wobblin' 'long unsteady.

Summer day a-growin' old
    As the crimson sun is sinkin';
River sparklin' jest like gold
    Where the thirsty herd is drinkin'.
Cook a-yellin' "Grub-pile, boys!"
    Cups an' ol' tin plates a-rattle;
Punchers makin' lots o' noise
    On the bed-ground with the cattle.

$$\bullet \ \bullet \ \bullet \ \bullet \ \bullet$$

Silence on the midnight air!
    Me on night-herd slowly moggin
'Round the bedded cattle there,
    Singin' to 'em as I'm joggin'.
Campfire twinklin' down below;
    River sort o' lullabyin'
To the sleepers, soft an' low,
    In their blanket-beds a-lyin'.

Second watch a-rollin' out,
    Sleepy-eyed, with grimy faces,
At the foreman's lusty shout,
    Saddlin' up to take our places.
Me a-drowsin' off to rest
    With the starry orbs above me;
        Thoughts of You within my breast,
Dreamin', dreamin' that You love me!

"Old Six-Gun"

You've been a good old pal to me
    In all the years gone by;
You've saved my skin in many a spree,
    When Death was lurkin' nigh;
You're rusted some an' battered, too,
    But I ain't knockin' none,
'Cuz they's a heap I owe to you,
    You handy ol' six-gun!

I packed you on the cattle trail
    'Way back in '86,
An' never knowed you yet to fail
    When I got in a fix.
You've shot the lights out more'n once
    When we struck town fer fun,
An' done a heap o' them fool stunts,
    You handy ol' six-gun!

When my ol' paws close on yer grip,
    I seem to see once more
The prairie stretches in The Strip,
    An' the ol' bunkhouse door
Where night-times we would sit an' gaze
    Off to'rds the settin' sun—
Oh, wasn't them the happy days,
    You handy ol' six-gun?

I mind them nights we stood on guard
    When we was trailin' steers,
When growlin' thunder ripped an' jarred
    An' grumbled in our ears.
An' how that stampede made us sweat!
    'Twas sure a lively run!
You barked a-plenty then, you bet,
    You handy ol' six-gun!

An' now you're hangin' on the wall,
  Where firelight shadows play;
I reck'n, takin' all in all,
  That you hev seen your day.
But when I think what you've been through,
  An' all you've seen an' done,
A million plunks would not buy you,
  You handy ol' six-gun!

His Cowgirl Sweetheart

Ain't she jest a beauty, stranger?
    Slickest one in all the bunch.
Best of all she says she loves me,
    An' I've cottoned to the hunch.
She's my little cowgirl—savvy?
    With a heart that's true an' pure;
Got her corraled, roped an' branded,
    Yes, an' hog-tied, stranger, sure!

Gosh! she was a little vixen
    When I shied a rope at her!
Pawed an' snorted like tarnation,
    Bucked like all possessed—yes, sir!
Had to use some slick palaver
    'Fore I got my noose on tight;
That's her lopin' off—say, stranger,
    Ain't she simply out o' sight?

Ride? They's nothin' that's a-runnin'
    On four legs that she cain't ride!
Ought t' see her sit a saddle
    When she's lopin' at my side!
Thar's some class to what she hands 'em;
    On yer life, she cain't be beat;
Things move *mucho pronto*—savvy?
    When she warms a saddle-seat!

Mavericked 'round the range dern lonely
    'Fore I cut her from the herd;
Shied around her mighty keerful,
    'Fraid t' say a cussed word.
Didn't savvy all her chaffin'
    Till I saw her glad eyes shine
With the love-light that was in 'em,
    Then I knowed that she was mine!

Ain't she built fer keeps? You betcher!
  Talk about yer slick ones—say!
Trim an' natty as they make 'em,
  She's a sure swell looker—hey?
Got a step light as a fairy's,
  Eyes jest like twin jeweled stars;
Thar she is—that's her a-smilin'
  At me from the corral bars!

The Last Drive

Beside his sagging door he sits and smokes,
And dreams again of old trail days, long gone.
His eyes are dim; his form is bent and old,
And silvered are the locks about his brow.
He hears again the thud of pony-hoofs,
The clash of horns, the bellowing of herds;
The shout of riders and the pant of steeds,
And creak of saddle-leather as they ride.
He sees the dust-clouds hover o'er the trail
Where, snaky-like, the herd winds on and on;
He sees broad-hatted men, bronzed, fearless, bold,
And as he listens, faintly to his ears
Is borne the echoes of an old trail song,
While to his nostrils floats the scent of sage
And greasewood, cactus and mesquite, that seems
To lure him back among his ranges wide.

'Tis night! And now he sees the bedded herd
Beneath the studded canopy of heaven,
While hardy night-guards keep their vigil drear.
The stars gleam out, and yonder rocky buttes
Loom strange and weird and dim and spectral-like;
The wagon top shines brightly by the stream,
And in the flickering campfire's feeble glow
He sees the silent forms of old range pals
In dreamless slumber in their blanket beds.
The coyote's melancholy wail floats in
Upon the silent, pulseless summer air,
While overhead, on steady, tireless wing,
The night-hawk whirls and circles in its flight,
And down below, the babble of the stream
Makes low-crooned, soothing music rippling by.

Morn comes, with crimson bars of light that leap
To gild the buttes and tint the east with fire;
The lark's song echoes clear and sweet and strong
Upon the morning air; the range-grass gleams
And glitters with its diamond-tinted dew,
And all the great wide prairie springs to life.

Again he sees the straggling herd move on
In broken line, and in his dreams he seems
To feel the bronco's tireless, steady pace
That carries him upon his last long drive
Which ends in sleep along the Sunset Trail.

A Range Rider's Appeal

Guard me, Lord, when I'm a-ridin'
    'Crost the dusty range out there,
From the dangers that are hidin'
    On the trails, so bleak and bare.
Keep my stumblin' feet from walkin'
    In the quicksands of distress,
And my outlaw tongue from talkin'
    Locoed words of foolishness.

When around the herd I'm moggin'
    In the darkness of the night,
Or 'crost lonely mesas joggin'
    With no one but You in sight,
Won't you ride, dear Lord, beside me,
    When I see the danger sign,
And through storm and stampede guide me,
    With Your hand a-holdin' mine?

May the rope of sin ne'er trip me
    When to town for fun I go;
Let the devil's herders skip me
    On their round-ups here below.
May my trails be decked in beauty
    With the blossoms of Your love;
May I see and do my duty,
    Ere I ride the range above.

Let me treat my foes with kindness;
    May my hands from blood be free;
May I never, through sheer blindness,
    Git the brand o' Cain on me.
On the range o' glory feed me;
    Guide me over draw and swell,
And at last to heaven lead me,
    Up into the Home Corral.

The Lure Of The West

I want to go back where the greasewood grows,
 And the sagebrush smell is rank and sweet;
Where the desert wind o'er the mesa blows,
 And the buttes and sand-dunes my vision greet.
I want to forget the sight and sound
 Of city traffic and city roar,
And hurry away to my stamping-ground
 In God's great open—the West—once more.

I want to get out where the morning sun
 Shines warm on the broken buttes so strange,
And ride and ride where the cattle run
 On the dusty trails of the open range.
I'm sick of the streets and the lofty walls,
 Dark, barrier-like, on every hand,
The lure of the West—God's country—calls,
 And I'll go back to my desert land.

Again I list to the pine tree's croon,
 And the mystic murmur of mountain streams,
Which sing to me in the old, sweet tune
 I knew when dreaming my boyhood dreams.
The old log cabin, with sagging sill,
 The wide fireplace and the puncheon floor—
The vision gives me a homesick thrill,
 For Mother stands at the cabin door!

The lure of the West! There's a charm and spell
 That weaves a web with each passing hour,
With a subtle cunning that none can tell
 Who never have felt its magic power.
And I'll go back to my crags and peaks,
 To my great free plains and the brown earth's
  breast,
For the voice of Nature—God's creature—speaks,
 And wins me back to my love—the West!

A Cattle Range At Night

The prairie zephyrs have dropped to rest,
   And the dust-clouds settle down;
The sun dips low in the golden west,
   O'er the mesa bare and brown.
The wearied riders come loping in,
   As the hills grow dim and strange,
And the songs of the insect world begin—
   'Tis night on a cattle range.

The stars gleam out in the calm, clear sky
   Like twinkling orbs of light,
And over the range drifts the coyote's cry
   Through the star-lit summer night;
The night-hawk whirls in its ceaseless rush,
   As the evening breeze is stirred,
And the cowboy's song breaks the lonely hush,
   As he circles the bedded herd.

The campfire throws but a fitful glare,
   And the buttes like specters, rise
Far over the deep arroyo there,
   As sentinels in the skies.
While the silent forms in their blanket beds
   Dream on, to the night wind's sigh,
As gently about their sleeping heads,
   The breeze drifts idly by.

The moon steals up o'er the dark butte's crest
   In silvery shafts, which gleam
And sparkle there on the brown earth's breast
   Like gems in a fairy dream.
The night creeps on, with its mystic charms,
   To the song of the whip-poor-will,
And drifts to Dreamland in Nature's arms,
   And the range grows hushed and still.

The Old Line Shack

There wasn't much style about it;
    It hadn't a polished floor,
But only the rough-hewn lumber
    For walls, with a puncheon floor.
It stood on a treeless prairie,
    Far, far from the beaten track;
'Twas the cowpuncher's habitation,
    Was the Three-Circle old line shack.

'Twas the rudest of western cabins,
    Far out where the range-lands roll,
But its comfort and cheer oft sheltered
    Full many a kindly soul.
And many a night I've listened
    As the fitful breeze flung back
The sound of the coyote's wailing,
    In the Three-Circle old line shack.

Oh, many a trail song echoed
    Up over its rafters there,
Where the curling smoke-wreaths circled
    In the firelight's ruddy glare;
And many a thrilling story
    Was tuned to the rifle's crack,
In the days of the border troubles,
    In the Three-Circle old line shack.

We welcomed each chance acquaintance,
    And gave him a cheery hail;
We sheltered the cowboy stranger
    Who rode up the cattle trail.
The latch-string was ever hanging,
    And never a soul turned back
Who sought for a meal or blanket,
    In the Three-Circle old line shack.

I've lived in palatial mansions,
     Where comfort and wealth were spread;
Where tapestries hung, and clustered
     Themselves 'round my downy bed;
But oh, for those days Back Yonder,
     On Time's ever-changing track,
With my pardners who rode the ranges
     From the Three-Circle old line shack!

To An Old Branding Iron

You're a warped and rusty relic of the days of Long Ago,
    Ere the foot of Progress entered where you ruled with iron
        hand;
You are of an age departed; of an epoch none may know
    Who have never watched the conquest that you made
        throughout the land.
You have blazed the way for nesters who have turned their
    furrows deep
    Where the great herds roamed the prairies when you held
        unruffled sway;
You have seen advancing thousands with their goods and chattels
    creep
    Out across the dusty ranges where the cattle chose to stray.

You were pioneer and master in a region wild and rough;
    You were monarch in a section where a six-gun was the law;
You were backed by men of action, who were made of sterner
    stuff
    Than the country to the eastward of their ranges ever saw.
You have seen the cattle barons waxing rich in cows and steers
    From the brand you burned upon them in the dusty old
        corral;
For you were the leading factor in the West for thirty years
    Ere the nesters claimed the country you had ruled so long
        and well.

On a thousand hills were cattle that had felt your smoking brand,
    And the draws and coulees echoed with the bellowing of
        herds;
And they plowed a trail behind them as they straggled through
    the land,
    Urged by sinewy cowpunchers who were careless with their
        words.
By the onward march of Progress were your conquests held for
    naught;
    And you saw the herds forced slowly from the lands which
        you had won;

You have bowed to plow and reaper, which intruded where you
  fought,
And have watched your thousands scatter toward the far-off
  setting sun.

But the cattle trails are grassy, and the herds no longer roam
  Through the lands you fought to conquer from a subtle,
    cunning foe;
For the nesters came and fenced it, and the spot you knew as
  home
  Had no ties to hold you longer, and you gladly chose to go.
Rippling seas of grain now ripen where the puncher rode the
  range,
  And the hills no longer echo to his lusty shout, long-drawn;
You were forced to yield to Progress, with her customs new and
  strange;
  You're a warped and rusty relic of a life forever gone!

Out In The Golden West

Hearts are sturdy and strong and true,
    Out in the Golden West.
Cares and sorrows are mighty few,
    Out in the Golden West.
Business goes with a rush and rustle;
Everybody is on the hustle;
Life is teeming with go and bustle,
    Out in the Golden West.

Men are willing to take a chance,
    Out in the Golden West.
There is plenty of gay romance
    Out in the Golden West.
Maybe folks are a trifle rougher;
Some, perhaps, are a trifle tougher,
But they are quick to call a bluffer,
    Out in the Golden West.

Oh, but the life is broad and free,
    Out in the Golden West.
Plenty of show for you and me,
    Out in the Golden West.
There's where the skies are bluer, clearer;
There's where friendships are truer, dearer;
Heaven itself seems a trifle nearer,
    Out in the Golden West.

There is a tang to the mountain air,
    Out in the Golden West.
Nature's beauties are everywhere,
    Out in the Golden West.
Mountain peaks seem to loom up higher;
Of their grandeur we never tire;
It is the Land of Heart's Desire,
    Out in the Golden West.

Somehow we love it the more we stay,
    Out in the Golden West.
Grips us tighter from day to day,
    Out in the Golden West.
Mountain, canyon and prairie hold us;
Mother Nature leans to enfold us;
Yes, 'tis better than what they told us,
    Out in the Golden West.

Standing On His Merits

It's many a time I've plugged the lights,
    An' shot holes through the bar,
When I've rid in to see the sights
    From off the range afar.
I've nicked the tenderfoot's bootheels
    With bullets from my gun,
But I ain't been mixed up in deals
    Where killin' must be done.

I know I've painted things some red
    When I've come off the range,
An' sometimes I hev lost my head,
    An' acted wild an' strange.
I've rid my hawss in through the door
    To git somebody's goat,
But one thing I ain't done, fer shore—
    I never sold my vote!

You cain't blame me fer gittin' gay,
    An' playin' my best cyards,
When I've spent many a lonesome day
    With steers an' cows fer pards.
I may hev made a dern big noise,
    An' yelled to beat the band,
But I ain't never robbed the brays,
    Ner changed a cowman's brand!

I know I ain't no parlor gent—
    That ain't the range I browse—
But I ain't never stole a cent,
    Ner rustled no man's cows.
I reck'n I'm about as square
    As some swell guy of rank
Who's wanted by the sheriff there
    Fer bustin' up a bank!

The Dying Cowboy

Ol' pal, I'm goin' away off yonder,
    To the country that borders the Great Divide,
An' I've been dreamin' an' tried to ponder
    What's lyin' there on the other side.
Do the hardy fellows who ride its ranges
    Strike trails o' peace in its valleys fair,
Without no blizzards nor weather changes,
    Or wild stampedes on its mesas there?

I wonder, too, if the skies are bluer
    Than those that shelter us here below?
And the Round-Up Boss—is he any truer
    Than Jim or Billy, I'd like to know?
Is there any chance of a gun perceedin',
    Or don't six-shooters come into play?
I reck'n p'raps, that we're ruther needin'
    To know the Bible an' how to pray.

Shall I pack my chaps an' my spurs an' saddle,
    My ol' sombrero an' blue wool shirt?
Er don't the broncs that we'll hafto straddle
    On heaven's ranges, know bit or quirt?
I s'pose there's never no quicksands lyin'
    Around the streams of that golden land,
An' never a howlin' gale defyin'
    The heart an' nerve of its angel band.

They say there's nothin' but peace an' gladness
    A-waitin' there for the boys who go,
'Cuz the gospel-sharps say there ain't no badness
    Like that on this earthly range below.
It looks to me like a sure-'nuff winner,
    They's no night-ridin' to be gone through,
An' though you're branded a low-down sinner,
    The Foreman's waitin' to welcome you.

Bend low, ol' pal, for a misty shimmer
    Is dimmin' my eyes, an' I seem to see
That heaven range through the dusky glimmer,
    An'—hark! 'tis the Foreman a-callin' me!
The songs of the angel-band so tender
    Drift softly down through the chaparral;
Good-by, ol' pal, we will meet Up Yender,
    At the bars of the heavenly Home Corral!

"Sheeped Out"

It wasn't very long ago we bossed the ranges wide;
Our cattle wandered to and fro across the great divide.
We roamed its broad and beaten track with all our kith and kin,
But now we're bein' crowded back—the woolly-backs are in.

For it's bleat, bleat, bleat!
Can't you hear 'em up the trail?
They're croppin' all the herbage off
From coulee, hill and swale.
The sullen herder follows on,
And though he travels slow,
It looks as if the fates decreed
The cattle man must go!

We won the West from savage bands, in many a bloody deed,
And blazed our trails across its lands and tamed 'em for our need;
We was the pioneers of all, and though our style was rough,
While we could hear our cattle call, the West was good enough.

But it's bleat, bleat, bleat!
Now the woolly backs are here!
They're crowdin' in upon the range
We've held from year to year.
We fought to git the lands we love,
And now we stand no show;
Our herds are gittin' pushed aside;
The cattle man must go!

Already we've been forced along the range from state to state,
By that blamed idiotic song the cattlemen all hate;
The bobbin' lines of woolly-backs are stretchin' far away,
And we must quit our lands and shacks and seek new range today.

For it's bleat, bleat, bleat!
And a trail o' dust below!
The woolly-backs are crowdin' us,
And we have got to go.
We love the land we fought to win;

It's our'n alone by right,
But we are fadin' with our herds,
And driftin' out o' sight!

My Old Sombrero

Comrade of frontier glories,
    Relic of old trail days,
Battered and weather-beaten,
    Over the rough-hewn ways,
Bringing the breath of prairies,
    Silvered with morning dew—
Here's to you, old sombrero,
    Here is a toast to you!

Ah, but sweet memories linger
    Over your well-worn crown,
Fragrant with sage and greasewood,
    Out on the mesas brown!
Hark to the trail-songs yonder,
    Sung by a round-up crew!
Here's to you, old sombrero,
    Visions so dear of you!

Out of the dust-clouds rising,
    Straggles a trail-herd slow,
Winding in snaky column,
    Out to the plains below.
There is a glimpse of coulees
    Blossomed with flowers new—
Memories, old sombrero,
    Memories sweet of you!

There in your dingy likeness,
    Bringing a dream of home,
Thinking of bunkhouse pardners,
    Out where the longhorns roam.
Here where the firelight glistens,
    Memories we'll renew,
Graven, my old sombrero,
    Deep in the heart of you!

Musty and gray and drooping,
    You hang on your rusty nail,
Only an old-time relic,
    A dream of the cattle trail.
But oh, how the heart-beat quickens,
    And visions come crowding fast,
When I look at you, old sombrero,
    And think of the happy Past!

His Trade-Marks

The cowboy ain't no dandy
    When it comes to wearin' clo'es;
But when he trails to the city,
    He'll go as other folks goes.
But there's just two things he's wearin'
    From which he never scoots—
He'll stick to his old sombrero,
    He'll stick to his high-heeled boots!

He'll tackle a stranglin' collar
    That's hitched to a stiff b'iled shirt;
He'll discard his chaps and gauntlets,
    And wash off the prairie dirt;
But he'll hang to two possessions,
    Though folks turn up their snoots—
He'll stick to his old sombrero,
    He'll stick to his high-heeled boots!

He'll peel off his old bandana,
    And his overalls, too, he'll drop,
And he'll wear store duds and neckties,
    And his old blue shirt he'll swap.
But for just a part of his outfit
    He never has substitutes—
He'll stick to his old sombrero,
    He'll stick to his high-heeled boots!

He'll part his hair in the middle,
    And with perfume adorn his pelt;
He'll put on some real suspenders,
    Instead of a ca'tridge belt.
He'll lay off the gun he's wearin'
    But in spite of the jeers and hoots,
He'll stick to his old sombrero,
    He'll stick to his high-heeled boots!

Oh, yes, he's a queerish mixture
    When in from the range he strays,
And puts on a town man's toggin's,
    And copies the town man's ways.
But when to the town he's comin'
    To mix with the dude recruits,
He'll stick to his old sombrero,
    He'll stick to his high-heeled boots!

A Corral Soliloquy

You've been roped an' saddled an' bridled an straddled;
    I've spurred you an' quirted you, too;
You squealed an' cavorted; you sunfished an' snorted,
    As 'round the corral we both flew.
Your temper is sassy; your actions is classy;
    For buckin' you've sure got an itch;
I've swore I will bust you so that I kin trust you,
    So Pitch, you ol' pie-biter, pitch!

Your eye is afire with one bad desire—
    To git me down there in the dirt!
Go to it, ol' feller; there's no streak o' yeller
    Beneath my ol' blue flannel shirt!
I've met you an' matched you; I've larruped and
        scratched you;
    You cain't pile me there in the ditch!
You won't be the winner, you buck-jumpin' sinner,
    So Pitch, you ol' pie-biter, pitch!

You're gruntin' an' lungin' an' squealin' an' plungin',
    An' corkscrewin' 'round like a top;
You'd sure like to eat me, but you cain't unseat me;
    I'll ride you, ol' hawss, till you drop!
You are a jim-dandy; you're tough an' you're sandy;
    The way you go to it is rich;
So keep on a-humpin' yer back up an' jumpin',
    An' pitch, you ol' pie-biter, pitch!

You're gittin' some wheezy; you don't find it easy
    To rattle this whoopin' cowpunch!
In spite of your kickin' you'll find me still stickin',
    So lemme jest hand you this hunch:
You ain't the fust disgusted cayuse I've busted,
    An' rode to a frazzle an' sich;
If you only knew it, you gotta come to it,
    So pitch, you ol' pie-biter, pitch!

The Bunkhouse Boys

Who are a mighty happy crew
    In everything they say and do?
The wildest bunch I ever knew—
    The bunkhouse boys.

Who, though their manners may be rough,
    Are true as steel—the pure gold stuff,
And mighty quick to call a bluff?
    The bunkhouse boys.

Who ride the ranges, lone and drear,
    And herd the bawlin', restless steer
Through storm and sunshine, year on year?
    The bunkhouse boys.

Who ride through town to have their fun,
    With foamin' broncos on the run,
And smoke a-spittin' from each gun?
    The bunkhouse boys.

Who paint the place a lurid red,
    When decent folks are all in bed?
The bunch that's allus raisin' Ned—
    The bunkhouse boys.

Who blow their hard-earned ducats in
    At playin' poker—lose or win,
And take their losses with a grin?
    The bunkhouse boys.

When they ain't broke, who allus lends
    A five or ten-spot to their friends,
An' don't expect no dividends?
    The bunkhouse boys.

Who are the kings of sagebrush land,
   And allus give the glad, glad hand?
The crowd that wears the true-blue brand—
   The bunkhouse boys.

Back To Arizona

Take me back to Arizona as it was in early days,
Ere the cowboy on the ranges had the moving-picture craze.
Let me see the festive puncher with his bronco on the run,
Coming into town and shooting up the landscape with his gun.
Let me see the chuckawalla and the Gila monster, too,
Of the murderous Apache let me get a fleeting view;
Let me see a frontier squabble as it was in days of yore,
When the "bad man" of the border waded in a sea of gore.

Take me back to Arizona and the plains of alkali;
On the cactus-covered mesa in the desert let me lie;
Let me hear the rattler rattling as he crawls about the sand,
And the restive cattle bawling as they feel the red-hot brand.
Let me see the city marshal make a gun-play in the street,
And a victim later buried with his boots upon his feet;
Take me back to Arizona; let me see a poker game
As in days when it was prudent not to ask a stranger's name.

Take me back to Arizona, where they "sized" a fellow, not
By the boodle which he carried, but the skill with which he shot;
Where the towns were short on water, but all-fired long on gin,
And there never was much mourning when a fellow-man "cashed
    in."
Take me back among the ki-yotes and the centipedes and such,
Where a brand-iron was respected and a "rustler" hated much;
Take me back to Arizona when it lived a wild career,
And they had a man for breakfast every morning in the year!

Take me back to Arizona—Arizona rough and wild,
Where the days were dry and dusty and the whiskey wasn't mild;
Let me live again those stirring frontier days when all was new,
When the faro banks were frequent and the churches mighty few.
Let me join a sheriff's posse and get on a horse thief's track,
When a hanging-bee was likely if they brought the fellow back.
Take me back to Arizona in the palmy days I saw,
When high bootheels were in fashion and a six-gun was the law!

The Old Yellow Slicker

How dear to my heart was that old yellow slicker,
    I carried 'way back in my cowpunchin' days;
'Twas stiff as a board, but I wasn't a kicker
      When it was a-rainin' an' me huntin' strays.
I carried it tied at the back of my saddle,
    All ready for blizzard or windstorm or rain,
An' 'twas my salvation when I had to straddle
      My bronc' an' lope out on the mud-spattered plain.
        That old yellow slicker,
        That spacious old slicker,
    I carried on many a round-up campaign!

That old yellow slicker! 'Twas big an' 'twas roomy;
    It sure kept me dry when the rain trickled down;
I wore it on night-herd with skies black an' gloomy,
      It covered me well from my feet to my crown.
No matter how sloppy or muddy or lowery;
    No matter how cold or unpleasant the storm,
No matter how blusterin', gusty or showery,
      That old yellow slicker I wore kept me warm!
        That ill-fittin' slicker,
        That fish-oil-soaked slicker,
    Its mission it never yet failed to perform.

That old yellow slicker which I have defended,
    Hangs there in the bunkhouse agin the log wall;
Its mission's fulfilled, an' its range life is ended—
    No more do the herds on the cattle-trail call.
But sometimes I dream in the dim summer gloamin',
    An' there in the embers which flicker an' change,
I catch a faint glimpse of the herds that were roamin',
    An' think of that slicker I wore on the range.
        That battered old slicker,
        That old yellow slicker,
    A cattle-day relic I'll never exchange!

The Short-Grass Country

Out in the short-grass country,
    Out where the greasewood grows;
Out where the ki-yote hollers,
    Out where the blizzard blows!
That is the place I'm seekin',
    That is the land for me,
      Ridin' a-straddle
      A cowpunch saddle,
    Over the sagebrush sea!

Out in the short-grass country,
    Out on the mesas brown,
Far from the rush and worry,
    Far from the haunts of town.
Out where it's peace and quiet,
    Restful and calm and free,
      Ridin' a-straddle
      A cowpunch saddle,
    Over the sagebrush sea!

Out in the short-grass country,
    Out where yer pals are true;
Drinkin' the glorious sunshine,
    Under the skies of blue.
Out of yer tarp at daylight,
    Frisky as you can be,
      Ridin' a-straddle
      A cowpunch saddle,
    Over the sagebrush sea!

Out in the short-grass country,
    Out where there's room to spare;
Out where no smoke's pollutin'
    The fresh-blown prairie air.
Out where no street-kyars bother,
    Out where yer safe, by gee!
        Ridin' a-straddle
        A cowpunch saddle,
    Over the sagebrush sea!

Out in the short-grass country!
    Pardner, say, ain't it fine?
Livin' in perfect freedom,
    Out where the air's like wine.
Nothin', you bet, can beat it!
    Life is a jubilee,
        Ridin' a-straddle
        A cowpunch saddle,
    Over the sagebrush sea!

The Cowgirl

She ain't inclined to'rds lots o' things
 That eastern gals can do up brown;
She don't wear jewelry and rings,
 Like them swell girls what lives in town;
Her cheeks are tanned an olive tint,
 That shows the roses hidin' there;
Her eyes are brown, and there's a hint
 Of midnight in her wavin' hair.

She don't go in for fancy hats;
 A wide-brimmed Stetson is her pet;
She has no use for puffs and rats;
 A harem skirt would make her fret.
She wears a 'kerchief 'round her neck;
 At breakin' broncs she shows her sand,
And at a round-up she's on deck,
 And twirls a rope with practiced hand.

She doesn't know a thing about
 Them motor cars that buzz and whirr,
But when she goes a-ridin' out,
 A tough cow-pony pleases her,
Her hands are tanned to match her cheeks;
 Her smile will start your heart a-whirl,
And when she looks at you and speaks,
 You love this rosy, wild cowgirl!

She never saw a tennis court;
 She don't belong to any club,
But she is keen to all range sport,
 And she's a peach at cookin' grub!
She couldn't win at playin' whist;
 She wouldn't think that bridge was fun,
But say, the *hombre* don't exist
 That beats her handlin' a six-gun!

I don t believe she'd make a hit
   At them swell afternoon affairs;
She wouldn't feel at home a bit;
   Them ain't the things for which she cares.
She ain't so keen as some gals is
   At tryin' stunts that's new and strange,
But you can bet she knows her biz
   When she's out on the cattle range!

The Man From Cherrycow

A new top hand blowed in today
    From down around the Cherrycow;
He started in to talk, and say—
    You'd thought nobody else knowed how
To pitch a rope or run a brand,
    Or handle any outlaw nag;
But he soon got to understand
    This cow camp wa'n't no place to brag!

He told about the rides he'd made
    On outlaws no one'd ever rode;
How he clumb on and how he stayed—
    That cuss from Cherrycow sure blowed!
He had us all backed off the map,
    And might have held the rep he claimed,
But for a fortunate mishap
    Which must have made him plumb ashamed.

Our foreman, Shorty Bates, says he:
    "That's some talk, stranger that you spring
Come down to the corral with me,
    And back up all them words you sling.
We got an ol' blue roan out here,
    And if you stick ten jumps on her,
You git a job right through the year
    A-breakin' broncs at sixty per."

The man from Cherrycow he laffed,
    And trailed off down to the corral,
While Shorty follered him and chaffed
    The Cherrycow bronc peeler well.
"I'll bet ten bones," says he, "right now,
    That I kin ride that bronc and stick."
And Shorty says to Cherrycow:
    "Here's ten that you cain't do that trick."

They roped the roan and cinched her tight;
    She bawled and bucked like all possessed;
But Cherrycow clumb on all right,
    With pride a-bulgin out his chest.

• • • • •

They're in the bunkhouse with him now;
    I reck'n doc'll pull him through,
But there's one man from Cherrycow
    Who bit off more'n he could chew!

The Grub-Pile Call

There's lots o' songs the puncher sang in roundin' up his herds;
The music wasn't very grand, an' neither was the words.
No op'ry air he chanted, when at night he circled 'round
A bunch of restless longhorns that was throwed on their bed-
    ground;
But any song the cowboy on his lonely beat would bawl,
Wa'n't half as sweet as when the cook would start the grub-pile
    call.

I've heard 'em warble "Ol' Sam Bass" for hours at a time;
I've listened to the "Dogie Song," that well-known puncher
    rhyme;
"The Dyin' Cowboy" made me sad, an' "Mustang Gray" brung
    tears,
While "Little Joe the Wrangler" yet is ringin' in my ears.
But of the songs the puncher sang, I loved the best of all,
That grand ol' chorus when the cook would start the grub-pile
    call.

There wasn't any sound so sweet in all the wide range land;
There wa'n't a song the puncher was so quick to understand.
No music that he ever heard so filled him with delight
As when he saw the ol' chuck-wagon top a-gleamin' white;
An' like a benediction on his tired ears would fall
The sweetest music ever heard—the welcome grub-pile call.

I've laid at night an' listened to the lowin' of the steers;
I've heard the coyote's melancholy wail ring in my ears.
The croonin' of the night-wind as it swept across the range
Was mournful-like an' dreary, an' it sounded grim an' strange.
But when the break o' day was near, an' from our tarps we'd
    crawl,
The mornin' song that charmed us was that welcome grub-pile
    call.

The Frontier Marshal

The frontier marshal wa'n't no saint,
    Nor weak-kneed cringin' cuss
Who'd knuckle down an' mebby faint
    If mixed up in a fuss.
The thing he allus learned well first
    Was how to turn a trick,
An' if the worst should come to worst,
    To just be trigger-quick.

He was a man who knew the art
    Of handlin' a six-gun;
An' when he had to play his part,
    He saw that 'twas well done.
He allus aimed to git his man,
    An' he shot quick an' straight,
Becuz 'twas apt to spoil his plan
    To be a second late.

He wasn't much on dress er looks
    Out in that frontier land;
He wasn't posted much on books,
    But he had nerve an' sand;
An' many a "bad man" of the plains
    Who crossed him in disputes,
Was quickly planted, for his pains,
    Still wearin' of his boots.

He was the majesty of law
    In them wild border days;
As quick as lightnin' on the draw,
    When mixed in shootin' frays.
So here's to him—that nervy gent,
    The frontier marshal bold,
Who knowed what real gun-fightin' meant
    In them rough days of old.

A Cowboy's Version

When I'm ridin' alone in the night-time way out on the desolate
range,
With the moon shinin' down through the cloud-hills and the
canyons and draws lookin' strange
And the shadowy buttes loomin' dimly, way out where the
coyotes call,
I know that the hand of no human conceived it and fashioned it
all.

When I'm lopin' across the wide mesa where blossoms send out
their perfume,
I know that an All-Wise Creator had somethin' to do with each
bloom;
'Cuz no mortal hand on this planet could paint us them colors, I
know,
Nor spangle the coulees and foothills with all the gay posies that
grow.

I know that the green of the ranges don't come at the biddin' of
man;
The landscape makes all of them changes because of the Creator's
plan.
I know that the beauties about me—the sunshine, the blooms and
the rest,
Wa'n't put there by man nor his helpers, but at the good Lord's
own behest.

And nights when I lie at the campfire and look at the stars in the
sky,
I'm ready to own that no human made all of them planets on
high;
But only the Boss of the Heavens reached down from the Home
Ranch above,
And moulded and builded and fashioned the blossoms and ranges
I love.

To His Cow Horse

You are homelier than sin;
    Wouldn't take no beauty prize;
You are scrubby an' you're thin,
    An' the devil's in your eyes.
But, ol' pal, I'd bank on you
    Over any thoroughbred,
'Cuz I know what you kin do
    When you take it in your head.

When I tackled you at first,
    You was somethin' on the pitch;
For awhile I got the worst
    When you'd land me in the ditch.
How you blatted an' you bawled
    In the dusty ol' corral,
When astride your back I crawled
    An' let out a cowboy yell!

There is ginger in you yet,
    Though you stand with droopin' ears;
Oh, you ain't no slouch, you bet,
    When it comes to partin' steers!
'Course you ain't so much on style,
    'Cuz you're rode an' larruped hard,
But I'd hunt a derned long while
    'Fore I found a better pard!

Though you're ugly as the deuce,
    When a mean streak's in your skin,
An' you sometimes jar me loose
    When them plunges you begin;
Though your looks don't cut much ice,
    You kin put this in your pipe—
Ain't nobody got your price,
    'Cuz you ain't for sale, by cripe!

Trouble For The Range Cook

Come wrangle yer bronco an' saddle him quick!
The cook is in trouble down there by the creek!
Oh, cinch up yer latigoes—all o' you runts,
An' pull 'em so tight that yer ol' bronco grunts.
'Twill need all the punchers the foreman can send,
'Cuz the chuckwagon's mired down there by the bend!

The cattle are scatterin' over the plain,
While punchers are yellin' in language profane!
But let 'em spread out—for the cook's in a muss,
An' quicksands are causin' the feller to cuss.
Oh, this is the time ev'ry puncher's his friend,
'Cuz the chuckwagon's mired down there by the bend!

Come on, with yer ropes that are heavy an' stout!
No grub for the bunch till the wagon's pulled out!
It's in to the hubs an' a-sinkin' down slow,
An' cookie is cussin' an' watchin' it go!
Come, hustle, you punchers an' haul him to land,
Before we are conquered by water an' sand!

A-strainin' of ropes an' a-gruntin' of nags,
An' woe to the puncher whose lariat sags!
It's spur 'em an' quirt 'em, an' make 'em lay to—
An'—now she is movin'! An'—now she is through!
It's worth all the time that the effort required,
'Cuz it's nothin' to eat when the chuckwagon's mired!

A Westerner

I knowed he was a Westerner,
    I knowed it by his talk;
I knowed it by his headgear,
    I knowed it by his walk.
His face was bronzed and fearless;
    His eye was bright and keen,
That spoke of wide, vast ranges
    I knowed that he had seen.

Somehow I knowed he'd ridden
    The range-lands of the West;
His speech was bunkhouse pattern—
    The kind I love the best.
He brought a hint of prairies,
    Of alkali and sage;
Of stretches wide and open—
    The Western heritage.

I knowed he was a Westerner
    Just from the way he done;
His footgear, too, proclaimed him
    A stalwart Western son.
He had "the makin's" with him,
    And I could not forget
His bed-ground from the manner
    He rolled his cigaret.

He brought with him the freedom
    Of that great Western land;
Where grassy billows, endless,
    Sprawl out on ev'ry hand.
The city noises chafed him,
    And each skyscraper tall
Seemed like grim barriers risin',
    Or some deep canyon wall.

He seemed a part and parcel
    Of countries wide and far,
Where great herds dot the mesas,
    Out where the cowmen are.
I knowed he was a Westerner
    Becuz he was so free
In yellin' "Howdy, pardner!"
    When he was passin' me.

Sence Slim Got "Piled"

Slim Bates ain't braggin' any more
    About how be kin ride;
An' gosh, but be gits mighty sore
    Whenever he is guyed.
He uster be so full o' vim,
    So reckless an' so wild,
But there's a change come over Slim
    Sence he got piled.

He uster tell of outlaw nags
    He'd gentled like a cow,
But Slim ain't makin' any brags
    Of tamin' outlaws now.
He's jest the humblest cuss, I swear,
    As meek as any child;
Slim dassn't even take a dare
    Sence he got piled!

Accordin' to Slim's flossy talk
    He was some cowpunch once;
The worst cayuse could pitch an' balk,
    An' try his wildest stunts;
But now Slim hangs his head in shame,
    For six weeks he ain't smiled;
Slim knows that he ain't in the game
    Sence he got piled.

Of course when he come driftin' in,
    We thought he knowed his biz;
We swallered all them yarns he'd spin
    'Bout ridin' stunts o' his.
But now we pass him up with scorn,
    He's all but plumb exiled;
Slim ain't a-tootin' of his horn
    Sence he got piled.

He's bogged hisself down good an' deep;
    He'd better drift along
An' git a job at herdin' sheep,
    'Cuz here he's in plumb wrong.
Nobody herds with Slim a bit,
    He's got this outfit r'iled;
He'll never hear the last of it
    Sence he got piled!

Autumn On The Range

Off across the wide arroyo, sweeps the breezes of the fall,
Where the haze of Injun summer sort o' lingers over all;
Ev'ry bronco is cavortin' in the chilly autumn air,
And the yippin' of their riders is resoundin' everywhere.

The campfire smoke is risin' sort o' lazy-like and slow,
Where the cook is busy mixin' up a batch o' sour-bread dough;
And the boys who rode on night-herd are a-yawnin' in their beds,
While the foreman showers cuss-words down upon their luckless
    heads.

There's a smell of fryin' bacon as it sizzles in the pan,
And the boys'll soon be lined up at the mess-box to a man;
And the cups'll be a-clatter, fer the coffee's b'ilin' hot,
While the slapjacks that are bakin' are a-goin' to hit the spot.

Soon the dust-clouds will be risin' where the herd is stragglin'
    through,
And there'll be some lively doin's by the hull blamed round-up
    crew;
There'll be runnin', there'll be dodgin' when they start to cuttin'
    out,
And the sagebrush flats will echo with the cowman's lusty shout.

So you'd better cord yer beddin' and then climb into yer chaps,
And when you hev gulped yer coffee, cinch yer latigoes and
    straps,
For they're drivin' in the hawss-herd and the puncher's day's
    begun,
And there's goin' to be some sweatin' 'fore the cuttin' out is done.

The Cattle Rustlers

Our stronghold lies where the plains are gashed,
  And the coulees twist and bend;
Where the brushy mesas are yet unslashed,
  And the buck-brush has no end.
And there we fly when the word comes back
That the cattle barons are on our track.

We take our toll from the herds that roam;
  From none do we stay our hand;
In the rolling hills we are right at home
  When changing another's brand.
We know the trails and each frowning butte,
And the rustler's quick on the draw and shoot.

We hold our lives in our hands each day,
  And Death stalks close by our side;
The rustler knows he is common prey
  Wherever the cowmen ride;
Short shrift indeed it will mean for him—
If he is caught, 'tis a noose and limb!

But the rustler's life is a life of ease,
  In the borders of Cattle Land.
With a speedy bronco between his knees,
  And a running-iron in his hand.
We take our toll without fear or fuss
That a sheriff's posse may capture us!

The "Finale" Of The Puncher

When the last great herd has vanished,
 And the open range is gone;
When the cattle all are banished,
 And their numbers are withdrawn,
When the brandin' days are over,
 And the ropin' all is through,
Then it is we'll sit and wonder
 What's the cowpunch goin' to do?

When the cowman comes to sever
 What connections he had left;
When the trail-herds pass forever,
 And there ain't a cayuse left;
When the ol' chuckwagon rumbles
 O'er the ridges out of view,
And the cook quits yellin' "Grub pile!"
 What's the puncher goin' to do?

When the squealin', buckin' bronco
 Has become an ol' plow nag;
When the saddle and the poncho
 Hang up in an ol' grain bag;
When his bits and spurs are rustin',
 And his gun is useless, too,
And there's no more round-ups startin'
 What's the puncher goin' to do?

When the last night-herdin's finished,
 And he's seen his last stampede,
When the bunkhouse gang's diminished,
 And of brand-irons there's no need;
When the ol' worn yellow slicker
 Is put by for store-duds new,
And his chaps have been discarded,
 What's the puncher goin' to do?

When there ain't no wild west longer;
    When the plains are seas of grain,
And the nesters crowd in stronger,
    Till the cowman can't remain;
When the ol' life's but a vision
    To which he must bid adieu,
Tell me, oh, my ol' range pardners,
    What's the puncher goin' to do?

Rainy Day In A Cow Camp

Gusty sheets o' rain a-fallin';
    Yellow slickers our attire;
Wet, bedraggled longhorns bawlin';
    Cook a-cussin' at the fire.
Grub all water-soaked an' soggy;
    Foreman's temper all a-flare;
Ev'ry puncher feelin' groggy;
    'Dobe stickin' ev'rywhere!

Broncos standin' heads a-droopin';
    All their ginger plumb soaked out;
Dumb to all the wrangler's whoopin',
    An' to ev'ry puncher's shout.
Saddles sloppy an' a-slippin';
    Cinches plastered full o' mud;
Ev'ry ol' sombrero drippin';
    'Royos roarin' with the flood.

Ol' cow hawss a-slippin', slidin'
    Up an' down the slushy hills;
Punchers all humped up a-ridin';
    Ev'ry minnit has its thrills.
Wind a-whistlin'; skies a-weepin';
    Slickers flappin' when we lope;
Rain inside our chaps a-creepin';
    Kinks an' knots in ev'ry rope!

Ev'rybody blue an' sour;
    Not a sign o' sun in sight;
Jest a steady, soakin' shower
    When we ride to camp at night.
Blankets sozzled, wet an mussy;
    Tarps all damp an' feelin' strange;
Ev'ry puncher mad an' cussy,
    Hopin' mornin' brings a change!

To A "Triangle" Calf

I chased you through the chaparral,
    And yelled until I'm hoarse;
I herded you to the corral,
    And you dodged back, o' course.
I pitched my rope straight for your feet,
    And then you took a fall;
The butcher says you're fit for meat,
    So bawl, consarn you, bawl!

You've roamed the range from sun to sun,
    And had the best o' feed;
You've frisked about and had your fun
    With others of your breed.
But now you're fat enough for veal,
    And wait the butcher's call;
You git the rough end of the deal,
    But bawl, consarn you, bawl!

My bronc' is just a shadow now
    From chasin' you around;
You had the darndest way somehow,
    Of gittin' over ground.
You're wearin' the "Triangle" brand,
    You're fat and sleek and all;
Veal calves like you is in demand,
    So bawl, consarn you, bawl!

I've cussed you high and cussed you low,
    Conhang your snow-white face!
I'd cut you out and back you'd go
    To give me one more chase.
I roped you then and had to laugh
    To see you flop and sprawl;
You're full o' ginger for a calf—
    Now bawl, consarn you, bawl!

It won't be long afore your skin
   Is hangin' up to dry;
I reckon that you'd best begin
   Your prayers before you die.
You've been cut out as fit to kill;
   You ain't a bit too small,
So if you simply WON'T keep still,
   Why, bawl, consarn you, BAWL!

Only A Bronco

I'm only a bronco, an unruly bronco,
    A range-ridden bronco, wild, scrubby and tough;
I'm bridled and saddled at daylight and straddled,
    I'm larruped and quirted and used mighty rough.
They slam and abuse me and daily misuse me,
    And when on the round-up I get little care;
I'm just a cow-pony, a pinto, and bony,
    But out on the ranges I do my full share.

I ain't no prize beauty, but I know my duty;
    I'm wise to the rope and the tricks of the trade;
You bet I'm no quitter; I'll hold any critter
    That you'll flip a rope on, for I ain't afraid.
No stall ever held me; they've always corraled me,
    I stand in the sun or the mud and the rain,
No roof to protect me, and though they neglect me,
    I'm only a bronco, and never complain.

Through coulee and hollow the cattle I'll follow,
    I chase 'em through buck-brush and sage and mesquite;
Down cut-bank and canyon my cowpunch companion
    Will recklessly urge me to head their retreat.
On night-herd I battle with stampeded cattle,
    That rush terror-stricken off into the gloom,
And sometimes I stumble, and then there's a tumble,
    And one more cowpuncher has gone to his doom!

Although you may doubt me, they can't do without me,
    In spite of the fact that my temper ain't mild.
I'm lively at pitchin' and always am itchin'
    To see the wild rider upon me get piled.
They never half feed me, for they're sure to need me
    Before I have browsed on the grass to my fill;
But though they deny me good care, they swear by me,
    And brag of my toughness and usefulness still.

I'm only a bronco, an ornery bronco,
   A range-ridden bronco with no pedigree;
I'm just a cow-pony, a pinto, and bony,
   But no hawss is wiser to range tricks than me.
No stall ever held me; they've always corraled me;
   I'm not of the breed of which hawss-raisers sing;
I'm long-haired and shaggy, tough-looking and scraggy;
   I'm only a bronco—just one of the string.

The Chisholm Trail

Where prairie breezes softly croon
    Across the ranges there,
I seem to hear a low, sweet tune
    Upon the balmy air;
It echoes softly as it strays
    Across each hill and swale,
And sings to me of frontier days
    Upon the Chisholm trail.

I look beyond, as in a dream,
    And seem to see again
The trail-herds by some sluggish stream,
    Just as I saw them then.
I see the drifting dust-clouds rise,
    And hear the cowman's hail,
As morning sunbeams tint the skies
    Upon the Chisholm trail.

The old chuckwagon top gleams bright;
    The campfire smoke I see,
As in the early morning light
    The "grub-pile" call rings free;
And from their "tarps" the punchers creep
    As morning stars grow pale,
And toss aside their dreams and sleep,
    To hit the Chisholm trail.

Grass-grown are now the trails we rode;
    The herds have all passed on;
Where once their teeming thousands flowed,
    The last longhorns are gone;
But 'round the campfire's cheery blaze,
    Full many a thrilling tale
Brings back to mind those frontier days
    Upon the Chisholm trail.

A Cowpunch Courtship

She got me clean stampeded
 An' locoed to a turn;
I oughtn't to have heeded
 Them fetchin' ways o' her'n.
I might have knowed for certain
 She'd git the bulge on me,
When I commenced a-flirtin'
 With her so all-fired free.

She was a peach, a pippin,
 An' 'twasn't nothin' strange
That I commenced a-skippin'
 Across onto her range;
I shouldn't gone cavortin'
 On her bed-ground, I know,
Head up an' jest a-snortin'
 To hog-tie her, you know.

You see at this here love-game
 I wasn't halter-broke;
'Twas new to me—this dove game,
 I liked it—that's no joke!
An' when I started chasin'
 Around in her corral,
'Twan't long 'fore I was facin'
 Conditions that was hell!

I told her I was ready
 To slap on her my brand,
She was close-herded steady
 By this love-sick cow-hand.
But jest when I was tryin'
 To slip on her my noose,
Why, she commenced a-shyin'
 An' framin' an excuse.

· · · · ·

The boys ain't quit their naggin';
        They're rubbin' on my raw;
My under lip is saggin'
        The wust you ever saw.
There's reason for it, maybe,
        But 'twon't occur again—
She's married, an' her baby
        An' ol' man's in Cheyenne!

The Range Cook's "Holler"

They sing of the puncher—that knight of the range who rounds
    up the bellerin' steer;
Who rides at the head of the midnight stampede with nary a
    symptom of fear;
They tell of his skill with the six-gun and rope, but nobody
    mentions the dub
Who trails the chuck-wagon through desert and plain and never
    yet failed with the grub!

The weather may find us in rain or in mud; may bake us or sizzle
    us down;
The treacherous quicksands may mire us deep, and the leaders and
    wheelers may drown;
The blizzards may howl and the hurricane blow, or Injuns may
    camp on our trail,
But nary excuse will the foreman accept for havin' the chuck-
    wagon fail.

For off on the range is the puncher who rides through buck-
    brush and sage and mesquite,
With an appetite fierce for the bacon we fry, and the slapjacks we
    bake him to eat.
And we must be waitin' with grub smokin' hot when he comes a-
    clatterin' in,
No matter what troubles we've bucked up agin, or what our
    delays may have been.

So in singin' yer songs of the men of the plains who trail it
    through desert and pine,
Who rough it from Idaho's borders clear down to the edge of the
    Mexican line,
Don't give all the due to the puncher of steers, but chip in some
    dope of the dub
Who trails the chuck-wagon in sun or in storm, and never yet
    failed with the grub!

A Child Of The Open

He is Nature's child and he's rough and wild—
    A son of the ranges wide;
Though he packs a gun he is keen for fun,
    When in from his herds he'll ride.
For, through and through, you will find him true,
    And kindly his keen gray eye,
And he'll serve a friend to the utmost end,
    Though doing it he may die.

For months he'll stay in the sagebrush gray,
    And mingle with cows and steers;
No welcome face 'round the whole derned place,
    Nor a woman's voice in his ears.
Though he isn't stuck on the tin can truck
    That the range cook feeds him there,
He doesn't frown as he gulps it down,
    As long as he gets his share.

In the mud and rain of the storm-swept plain,
    When the landscape is wet and blurred,
He rides and rides o'er the great divides,
    And watches the straggling herd.
In the glaring heat or the snow or sleet,
    When the blizzards howl and wail,
O'er draw and swell he guards them well,
    In the teeth of the blinding gale.

He comes to town with a thirst to drown,
    From months in the solitude;
He howls like sin, and he gets run in
    If he's scrappy or rough or rude.
But when he's free and has quit his spree,
    He'll strike for the range once more,
And the outdoor joys with the Two-Bar boys,
    And a bed on the bunkhouse floor.

Forest Conservation In Crimson Gulch

Woodman, spare that tree!
    Touch not a single bough!
We've cattle rustlers—three,
    To hang upon it now.
Oh, do not touch a limb,
    We're after Six-Gun Lew,
And when we capture him,
    He'll decorate it, too.

This tree in days of yore,
    Was old Judge Lynch's pride;
Up in its branches, more
    Than ten outlaws have died.
Train-Robber Bascom swung
    From that limb to his death;
Here Hoss-Thief Higgins hung
    Till he got short of breath.

In other days than these,
    Within this sheltered glade,
So many hanging bees.
    We held beneath its shade.
This oak we will defend;
    Tonight we storm the jail,
Take Quick-Shot Sparks and send
    Him o'er the dim Long Trail.

We pray that you will spare
    This hardy tree so dear,
For many a hemp affair
    Will be pulled off right here.
A sheriff's posse's out
    For Slim Bill's band, you see;
They'll want these limbs, no doubt,
    To hold a neck-tie spree.

Woodman, hack it not,
    For to this tree we cling!
Tomorrow night we've got
    Two bandits who must swing.
So spare these limbs, we pray,
    For it is our belief
This afternoon we may
    Hang that Bar-5 horse-thief!

A Locoed Outfit

The new schoolmarm on Bear Paw Creek
    Has rosy cheeks an' twinklin' eyes;
She's got my round-up crew lovesick;
    I never seen such locoed guys.

They want to shave now ev'ry day,
    An' ile their hair an' change their clo'es.
The round-up's workin' down this way,
    But they won't ride, I don't suppose.

Instid o' blowin' in their rocks
    Fer silver spurs an' guns an' things,
They buy b'iled shirts an' fancy socks,
    Store ties an' collars too, by jings!

I don't suppose it's nothin' strange,
    'Cuz gals is scarce around these parts;
Though she's ten mile across the range,
    She's sure stirred my cowpunchers' hearts.

If they go out a-huntin' strays,
    Er ridin' fence, they're sure to roam
To'rds Bear Paw Creek, to ride a ways
    With that there schoolmarm, goin' home.

They sure close-herd that schoolmarm gal;
    They're lovers that don't never shirk;
They hang around her home corral,
    An' do blamed little cowpunch work.

They moon around the bunkhouse door,
    Plumb jealous of each other, too;
I wish that gal would hike afore
    She hypnotizes 'em clean through!

Spring In Sagebrush Land

In Sagebrush Land it's Springtime, and the desert is a-bloom
With a weave of wondrous colors from old Mother Nature's
    loom.
Ev'ry bronco's feelin' lazy and inclined to want to shirk,
And us punchers have a feelin' we would ruther loaf than work.

We're a-lookin' for the round-up to be startin' pretty quick,
But you tell the boys about it and they all commence to kick;
'Cuz these balmy Springtime mornin's ev'rybody wants to doze,
And when we will start to gather up the cattle, goodness knows!

On the bunkhouse steps we gather when the mornin' sun is seen
Shinin' on the distant mesa where the grass is turnin' green,
And we sit and roll the makin's, idly talkin', as we drowse,
On all subjects under heaven but the one of steers and cows.

We had ought to be a-ridin' on the range a-huntin' strays,
But we're actin' like we're locoed these sunshiny Springtime days;
And the foreman is a-cussin' at the lazy way we do,
But the range is shy of punchers, and we guess he knows it, too!

Our saddles are a-hangin' in the bunkhouse on the wall,
But we only grunt o' mornin's when we hear the "cooky" call;
'Cuz in Sagebrush Land it's Springtime, and us punchers, in our
    hearts,
Feel that we don't care, by thunder, if the round-up never starts!

Bad Man Jones

Bad Man Jones he come to town
    To have his yearly spree;
Shot the hull place up an' down,
    An' sideways too, by gee!
He cowed the barkeep by one glance,
    An' plugged out all the lights,
An' made a Boston lunger dance,
    Who'd come to see the sights.

Bad Man Jones he took the place,
    An' run the marshal out;
Had the hull dern populace
    Plumb scart, they ain't no doubt.
He made us do jest as he'd choose,
    An when he ordered drinks,
They wasn't no one dast refuse
    To licker up, by jinks!

Bad Man Jones he sure was game,
    He plugged holes everywhere;
An' didn't stop to take no aim
    When smokin' up the air.
He shot the bootheels off'n some,
    An' laffed when they turned pale,
An' nary deputy dast come
    An' march him off to jail.

Bad Man Jones he swaggered 'round,
    A gun in either hand;
The sheriff tackled him an' found
    He hadn't lost his sand.
Bad Man Jones he fired one shot;
    The sheriff stopped the pill;
He's sleepin' in a shady spot
    Up there on Boneyard Hill!

Bad Man Jones he made us sweat,
  But now his reckerd's dim,
Becuz his wife, a suffragette,
  She got plumb after him.
She took his gun right on the spot,
  An' talked in thunder tones,
An' now the meekest man we got
  Is that same Bad Man Jones!

The Cowman's Saddle

It is big and wide and roomy, and it's solid, every bit,
And there's forty pounds o'substance in the makin' up of it;
It isn't nothin' fancy, 'cuz it ain't built fer display—
It is just the cowman's workshop where he spends a busy day.

The seat is smooth and shiny, and it's colored a rich brown,
'Cuz it's polished on the round-up, or when he rides in to town;
It gits bard knocks a-plenty, and it's out in rain and sun,
And it's throwed around permis'cus when the puncher's day is
     done.

The latigoes are heavy, and the cinches good and strong,
So there won't be nothin' bustin' if the cowman s work goes
     wrong;
And when he's settled in it, you can bet he makes things hum,
And whatever he should tie to when he's ropin', has to come.

When the old chuckwagon's mired and the cook begins to swear,
Then the puncher and his saddle and his rope are allus there;
When unlucky steers git foundered and are sinkin' in the sand,
'Tis the same old combination hauls the critters to dry land.

But you can climb astride it, and no matter where you go,
You will think you're in a cradle, cuz the motion soothes you so;
And when you have ridden in it for about a week, b'jing,
You will swear the cowman's saddle is about the proper thing!

The Call From The West

Where the grass-lands roll in stretches like an endless, tossing sea,
To the mountains white and hoary, over ranges wide and free,
Where the country lies unbroken, and soft prairie breezes blow,
It is there my heart turns fondly and the siren bids me go.

It is far from cares and worries and the sordid haunts of man,
And the ceaseless rush and turmoil of the money-making clan;
Only peace and gladness linger 'round its quiet solitudes,
For the grasping hand of Progress on its border ne'er intrudes.

My country fair and shining, lies where sunset's glory gleams,
Over mountain-tops and mesas and along smooth, winding
    streams.
Where the greasewood and the sagebrush fling their sweet
    perfume afar,
And the cow-men watch their trail-herds by the blazing evening
    star.

I see it every evening in the dreams which come to me—
My glorious Western homeland across the sagebrush sea!
It lures my thoughts off yonder, where soft the twilights fall,
Where hearts are true and tender, and prairie breezes call.

And I must rise and answer, for the lure is ever strong;
It calls and beckons to me and breathes the West's own song.
It sings of wide horizons and sunny skies and fair,
Which seem to smile upon me and turn my footsteps there.

The Cowboy

With eyes that were blazing,
But now that are glazing,
In barroom, "The Bruin"— that rattlesnake den—
A cowboy is lying,
And silent, is dying,
Surrounded by careless, yet resolute men.

So, sing of the rover,
Whose wand'rings are over,
And who, without even a tremor of dread,
Lies down on the prairie,
Where nature makes merry,
And spears of the cactus are guarding his bed.

Ho' father and mother,
And even one other,
Had begged him to tarry, they pleaded in vain;
For wild as a ranger,
And mocking at danger,
He cared but to gallop, a Knight of the Plain.

Tho' zephyrs were creeping,
Or tempests were leaping,
The spur, to the bronco, he wantonly prest;
And shouting and singing,
And lariat swinging,
Rode on like a spirit that never knew rest.

Wherever he wandered,
His money he squandered,
With hand of a gambler and kingliest grace;
And ever was willing
To stake his last shilling
On turn of a penny or chance of an ace.

A hand to the weary,
And smile to the dreary,
He willingly offered to lowliest woe;
And taunt to the sneering,
And blow to the jeering,
As willingly tendered to insolent foe.

Last night, at The Bruin,
He guzzled red ruin,
And tackled draw poker, along with the rest;
When one began stealing
The cards they were dealing,
And waddy objecting, was shot in the breast.

Aware that he's going,
For cold he is growing,
He calls for his saddle as rest for his head;
Then says, without flinching,
That "Death is now sinching,"
And then, on his blanket, the puncher lies dead.

So, sing in soft numbers,
Of him that now slumbers,
Who wantoned with fortune and scouted at care;
And sweetly is dreaming,
Tho' curlews are screaming,
And coyotes howling like imps of despair.

Ben

As many boys have longed to do,
  and many boys have done,
When in my teens, I drifted West,
  To find where wealth was won;
And anchored soon where men were tough,
  As tough as earth could boast,
Where each it seemed, had volunteered
  To serve in Satan's host.

Among the number there was one
  They called the "Devil's Ace,"
A fellow with a sorrel top,
  And yellow, freckled face;
Whose wrath was like the fiery floods
  That sweep the rolling plain,
With fury that no tongue may tell,
  Nor mortal arm restrain.

Another one was "Saintly Sam,"
  A coy, but gamey bird,
Who rarely steamed above his gauge,
  And rarer cussed a word;
And yet whose heart was like the wild,
  Where spears of cactus grow,
And he that dared to trespass there,
  Received a stinging blow.

And one was dubbed as "Whiskey Jack,"
  A brutal, brawling bloat,
Who'd meanly thump the tenderfoot,
  Then o'er his anguish gloat;
And there were Buck and Booze and Blood,
  Who had no thought of fame,
And yet, in way of wickedness,
  Deserved an honored name.

But there was one among the crowd,
    I only knew as "Ben;"
Who stood a notch above the rest
    Of all those rowdy men;
Who was a brawny, burly chap,
    The master soul of sin,
And where the others called a halt,
    He'd just about begin.

In every spree he'd be the one
    To down the most of budge;
And as to who had won at cards,
    He'd always be the judge;
In short, he was a Hercules,
    A sort of pagan boss,
Who made the other heathen bow,
    And worship him as Joss.

For such a harum-scarum lot
    Of course my gait was slow;
And then, I thought the track they took
    Was pointed straight below;
Besides, I'd vowed, when yet a kid,
    And pledged my mother, too,
That I would never taste the truck
    She said the demons brew.

It chanced the day I landed there,
    That some one set them up;
When I, with fears and yet with thanks
    Declined the proffered cup;
And then I thought my time had come,
    Because the others said,
That if I didn't hoist it in,
    They'd load my hulk with lead.

At this, big Ben—God save his soul!
  Stretched forth his arm of law,
And told each guzzler in the gang,
  To cease to wag the jaw;
And then he turned to me and asked,
  In way that sounded queer,
The why it was I then refused
  To take a drop of cheer.

Tho' fairly quaking in my boots,
  I yet had nerve enough,
To tell them why I'd vowed the vow
  To never taste the stuff;
And how, till then, I'd kept my word,
  In spite of jeer and scoff,
And therefore hoped they'd condescend
  To kindly let me off.

Then O, it seemed so good to hear
  The precious words of Ben,
As savagely, with blazing eyes,
  He faced the scowling men,
And swore, by all the blessed saints,
  He'd plug the imp of sin
Who dared to lay a hand on me
  To make me swig the gin.

And then, he said, in lower tones,
  A mother once he'd had,
Who tried her best, but died too soon,
  To raise a decent lad;
And then he hissed, between his teeth,
  He thought I'd acted square,
And that the whelp who disagreed,
  Would climb the golden stair.

And then the others called the turn,
    And said they wept for joy,
To find a chap— who hadn't wings—
    That yet was mother's boy;
Indeed, I guess, tho' strange it was,
    A couple even cried,
I reckon just because of her
    Who Ben declared had died.

And, odd to say, they caved around,
    With navy in each hand,
And said the one who filled me up,
    Would hunt the hotter land;
And odder too, they formed a ring,
    And raised their hands and swore,
That if I dared to break my pledge,
    They sure would hunt my gore.

As now I conjure back the scene,
    And live again the day,
That Ben stood there, and cussed and cussed,
    And kept those wolves at bay,
I swear he seems a Moses sent
    To sternly plead my cause,
And show to all those wretched men,
    The might of holy laws.

Just what the Lord should do with Ben,
    There is, of course, a doubt;
But still, I think, the righteous One,
    Should hardly bar him out;
At least, when I have reached the gate,
    Where Peter holds the key,
You bet your life I'll plead for Ben,
    As Ben once pled for me.

Maverick Joe

Don't know
Of Maverick Joe,
That buster of broncos in chief,
And who
As every one knew,
Waxed rich as a Maverick thief?

It's strange,
Out here on the range,
That you haven't known of his name,
Nor heard
How ranchers were stirred
Because of his Maverick fame.

Well, then,
I'll whisper again,
That tale of the cow and her kid,
Altho',
Thought Maverick Joe,
The trick was a corker they did.

Out West,
With lucre unblest,
He rangled for others a year,
While budge,
As well you may judge,
Occasion'ly offered him cheer.

One day,
With poker the play—
That game by no tenderfoot learned—
I hear
He rustled a steer,
That wasn't quite honestly earned.

And then,
He built him a den,
Way out where the punchers were few,
And there,
Tho' not by the square,
He soon to a cattle-king grew.

'Twas queer
How often that steer
Raised calves for his Maverick "+"(cross),
Tho' now,
I'm bound to allow,
His gain was some other one's loss.

One noon,
Along about June,
A Maverick daisy he saw—
The best,
And one that he guessed
He'd own by the Maverick law.

And so
He rastled it low,
And gave it a touch of his brand,
Then smiled,
For fortune beguiled,
That happiest chump in the land.

Next morn,
As sure as I'm born,
It chanced that a round-up begun,
And then,
Some blundering men,
Caught on to the caper he'd done.

For now,
They circled a cow,
One bearing "a " □ "(square) on her side,
That bawled,
And motherly called,
At sight of his Maverick pride.

The kid
Then bellowed and slid,
And buckled right in for a meal;
And—well,
It's idle to tell
The feelings he couldn't conceal

Tho' caught,
He swore it was bought,
Where never a seller was nigh;
But all,
Tho' praising his gall,
Yet reckoned no cattle would lie.

And thus,
That ornery cuss
Got sinched on account of that pair;
Because,
By cattlemen laws,
A "+" shouldn't tackle a " □ ".

The Cowboy Preacher

You may talk about the many
   In the race to gain the skies,
And may even name the sinners
   You declare to win the prize,
But if zeal, in matters holy,
   Can, for sin, at all, atone,
Bear in mind that bronco-riders
   Won't be last to reach the throne.

As you know, I left the college,
   In the spring of 'eighty-one,
With the wish to preach the Gospel,
   Out beneath the setting sun;
So, I wandered to the westward,
   Where the tide of empire rolls,
Seeking place to serve the Master,
   At the work of saving souls.

Well, by hap, the wheel of fortune,
   Steered me out upon the plain,
Where, it seemed, the mighty Reaper,
   Scarce would think to look for grain;
For the crop was thin and scanty,
   Yet would grow so very tall,
That, when Satan raised a tempest,
   It was sure to lodge or fall.

But, altho' the earth seemed arid,
   And, in spots, was nearly bare,
And, altho' the harvest Sower,
   Scattered wheat but here and there,
Still, the stalks, if few in number,
   Often gave a goodly yield,
Even tho' the storms of error,
   Swept, at times, across the field.

For the seed would never wither,
    Mattered not how poor the land,
As the lowly germs were planted,
    By a mother's magic hand;
And would therefore spring to beauty,
    In despite of drouths and rust,
And return a golden fruitage,
    For the garner of the Just.

And, of course, upon that prairie,
    On that wide and waveless sea,
Where the skies, in moving splendor,
    Span such vast eternity,
Man would grow in will and power,
    Man would gain in soul and brawn,
And the one, at heart, a coward,
    Found it best to gallop on.

Well, just why, I'll never tell you,
    But I liked those buccaneers,
Who so madly rode that ocean,
    In the wake of Texan steers;
So, I sharply veered my rudder,
    Fully bent to change my tack,
And was soon as wild a cowboy,
    As bestrode a bronco's back.

But, one day, the others reckoned—
    Just as tho' they didn't care—
That my gift was surely preaching,
    Seeing how I couldn't swear;
And, one eve, as fairy visions,
    From the past, came trooping in,
They declared it was my duty,
    There, with them, to wrestle sin.

Quickly, then, the touch of Conscience,
  Roused me from my slothful sleep,
While a spirit voice repeated
  Holy vows I'd failed to keep;
When, at once, with strange emotion,
  Moved, somehow, by wizard spell,
I arose and told the story,
  Each had heard his mother tell.

Cared I not, that hour, for glory,
  Spoke I not of carping creed,
Nor, to words of worldly wisdom,
  Gave I then a moment's heed;
But I simply led my hearers,
  'Mid the mob, beneath the tree,
Where the One, of love and mercy,
  Died, for them, on Calvary.

Ere my simple tale was finished,
  Many eyes were filled with tears,
And upon no lip was resting,
  E'en the trace of cynic sneers;
Later still, when praise was offered,
  Many sung that song of yore:
Come, ye sinners, poor and needy,
  Weak and wounded, sick and sore.

Now, it chanced that one, queer fellow,
  Left the crowd as I begun,
Stating that he choosed to vanish,
  Till that pious chap was done;
Whereupon the rest concluded,
  It was best to teach him, then,
That, when others talked religion,
  He should say, at least, "Amen."

So, when service all had ended,
    Plunged they him, by law of might,
In a pool of muddy water,
    Claiming thus they served him right;
And as forth he blindly scrambled,
    Of all sights about the worst,
Gave they him a second sousing,
    So he'd know he'd been immersed.

Therefore, when you count the many
    In the race to gain the skies,
And are pointing out the sinners,
    You declare to win the prize,
Bear in mind, if zeal is worthy,
    And, for sin, may e'er atone,
Then the rider of the bronco,
    Won't be last to reach the throne.

CHARLES BADGER CLARK, JR.

A Cowboy's Prayer
(Written for Mother)

Oh Lord. I've never lived where churches grow.
    I love creation better as it stood
That day You finished it so long ago
    And looked upon Your work and called it good.
I know that others find You in the light
    That's sifted down through tinted window panes,
And yet I seem to feel You near tonight
    In this dim, quiet starlight on the plains.

I thank You, Lord, that I am placed so well,
    That You have made my freedom so complete;
That I'm no slave of whistle, clock or bell,
    Nor weak-eyed prisoner of wall and street.
Just let me live my life as I've begun
    And give me work that's open to the sky;
Make me a pardner of the wind and sun,
    And I won't ask a life that's soft or high.

Let me be easy on the man that's down;
    Let me be square and generous with all.
I'm careless sometimes, Lord, when I'm in town,
    But never let 'em say I'm mean or small!
Make me as big and open as the plains,
    As honest as the hawse between my knees,
Clean as the wind that blows behind the rains,
    Free as the hawk that circles down the breeze!

Forgive me, Lord, if sometimes I forget.
    You know about the reasons that are hid.
You understand the things that gall and fret;
    You know me better than my mother did.
Just keep an eye on all that's done and said
    And right me, sometimes, when I turn aside,
And guide me on the long, dim trail ahead
    That stretches upward toward the Great Divide.

The Glory Trail

'Way high up the Mogollons,
    Among the mountain tops,
A lion cleaned a yearlin's bones
    And licked his thankful chops,
When on the picture who should ride,
    A-trippin' down a slope,
But High-Chin Bob, with sinful pride
    And mav'rick-hungry rope.

    "Oh, glory be to me," says he,
        "And fame's unfadin' flowers!
    All meddlin' hands are far away;
    I ride my good top-hawse today
    And I'm top-rope of the Lazy J—
        Hi! kitty cat, you're ours!"

That lion licked his paw so brown
    And dreamed soft dreams of veal—
And then the circlin' loop sung down
    And roped him 'round his meal.
He yowled quick fury to the world
    Till all the hills yelled back;
The top-hawse gave a snort and whirled
    And Bob caught up the slack.

    "Oh, glory be to me," laughs he.
        "We hit the glory trail.
    No human man as I have read
    Darst loop a ragin' lion's head,
    Nor ever hawse could drag one dead
        Until we told the tale."

'Way high up the Mogollons
    That top-hawse done his best,
Through whippin' brush and rattlin' stones,
    From canyon-floor to crest.
But ever when Bob turned and hoped
    A limp remains to find,
A red-eyed lion, belly roped
    But healthy, loped behind.

    "Oh, glory be to me," grunts he.
      "This glory trail is rough,
    Yet even till the Judgment Morn
    I'll keep this dally 'round the horn,
    For never any hero born
      Could stoop to holler: 'Nuff!'"

Three suns had rode their circle home
    Beyond the desert's rim,
And turned their star-herds loose to roam
    The ranges high and dim;
Yet up and down and 'round and 'cross
    Bob pounded, weak and wan,
For pride still glued him to his hawse
    And glory drove him on.

    "Oh, glory be to me," sighs he.
      "He kaint be drug to death,
    But now I know beyond a doubt
    Them heroes I have read about
    Was only fools that stuck it out
      To end of mortal breath."

'Way high up the Mogollons
    A prospect man did swear
That moon dreams melted down his bones
    And hoisted up his hair:
A ribby cow-hawse thundered by,
    A lion trailed along,
A rider, ga'nt but chin on high,
    Yelled out a crazy song.

"Oh, glory be to me!" cries he,
"And to my noble noose!
Oh, stranger, tell my pards below
I took a rampin' dream in tow,
And if I never lay him low,
I'll never turn him loose!"

Bacon

You're salty and greasy and smoky as sin
    But of all grub we love you the best.
You stuck to us closer than nighest of kin
    And helped us win out in the West.
You froze with us up on the Laramie trail;
    You sweat with us down at Tucson;
When Injun was painted and white man was pale
You nerved us to grip our last chance by the tail
    And load up our Colts and hang on.

You've sizzled by mountain and mesa and plain
    Over campfires of sagebrush and oak;
The breezes that blow from the Platte to the main
    Have carried your savory smoke.
You're friendly to miner or puncher or priest;
    You're as good in December as May;
You always came in when the fresh meat had ceased
And the rough course of empire to westward was
      greased
    By the bacon we fried on the way.

We've said that you weren't fit for white men to eat
    And your virtues we often forget.
We've called you by names that I darsn't repeat,
    But we love you and swear by you yet.
Here's to you, old bacon, fat, lean streak and rin',
    All the Westerners join in the toast,
From mesquite and yucca to sagebrush and pine,
From Canada down to the Mexican Line,
    From Omaha out to the coast!

The Westerner

My fathers sleep on the sunrise plains,
    And each one sleeps alone.
Their trails may dim to the grass and rains,
    For I choose to make my own.
I lay proud claim to their blood and name,
    But I lean on no dead kin;
My name is mine, for the praise or scorn,
And the world began when I was born
    And the world is mine to win.

They built high towns on their old log sills,
    Where the great, slow rivers gleamed,
But with new live rock from the savage hills
    I'll build as they only dreamed.
The smoke scarce dies where the trail camp lies,
    Till the rails glint down the pass;
The desert springs into fruit and wheat
And I lay the stones of a solid street
    Over yesterday's untrod grass.

I waste no thought on my neighbor's birth
    Or the way he makes his prayer.
I grant him a white man's room on earth
    If his game is only square.
While he plays it straight I'll call him mate;
    If he cheats I drop him flat.
Old class and rank are a wornout lie,
For all clean men are as good as I,
    And a king is only that.

I dream no dreams of a nurse-maid state
    That will spoon me out my food.
A stout heart sings in the fray with fate
    And the shock and sweat are good.
From noon to noon all the earthly boon
    That I ask my God to spare
Is a little daily bread in store,
With the room to fight the strong for more,
    And the weak shall get their share.

The sunrise plains are a tender haze
    And the sunset seas are gray,
But I stand here, where the bright skies blaze
    Over me and the big today.
What good to me is a vague "may be"
    Or a mournful "might have been,"
For the sun wheels swift from morn to morn
And the world began when I was born
    And the world is mine to win.

Ridin'

There is some that likes the city—
　　Grass that's curried smooth and green,
Theaytres and stranglin' collars,
　　Wagons run by gasoline—
But for me it's hawse and saddle
　　Every day without a change,
And a desert sun a-blazin'
　　On a hundred miles of range.

Just a-ridin', a-ridin'—
　　Desert ripplin' in the sun,
Mountains blue along the skyline—
　　I don't envy anyone
　　　　When I'm ridin'.

When my feet is in the stirrups
　　And my hawse is on the bust,
With his hoofs a-flashin' lightnin'
　　From a cloud of golden dust,
And the bawlin' of the cattle
　　Is a-comin' down the wind
Then a finer life than ridin'
　　Would be mighty hard to find.

Just a-ridin', a-ridin'—
Splittin' long cracks through the air,
　　Stirrin' up a baby cyclone,
　　　　Rippin' up the prickly pear
　　　　　　As I'm ridin'.

I don't need no art exhibits
　　When the sunset does her best,
Paintin' everlastin' glory
　　On the mountains to the west,
And your opery looks foolish
　　When the night-bird starts his tune
And the desert's silver mounted
　　By the touches of the moon.

Just a-ridin', a-ridin',
Who kin envy kings and czars
When the coyotes down the valley
Are a-singin' to the stars,
If he's ridin'?

When my earthly trail is ended
And my final bacon curled
And the last great roundup's finished
At the Home Ranch of the world
I don't want no harps nor haloes,
Robes nor other dressed up things—
Let me ride the starry ranges
On a pinto hawse with wings!

Just, a-ridin', a-ridin'—
Nothin I'd like half so well
As a-roundin' up the sinners
That have wandered out of Hell,
And a-ridin'.

The Bunk-House Orchestra

Wrangle up your mouth-harps, drag your banjo out,
Tune your old guitarra till she twangs right stout,
For the snow is on the mountains and the wind is on the plain,
But we'll cut the chimney's moanin' with a livelier refrain.

Shinin' 'dobe fireplace, shadows on the wall—
(See old Shorty's friv'lous toes a-twitchin' at the call:)
It's the best grand high that there is within the law
When seven jolly punchers tackle "Turkey in the Straw."

Freezy was the day's ride, lengthy was the trail,
Ev'ry steer was haughty with a high arched tail,
But we held 'em and we shoved 'em, for our longin'
    hearts were tried
By a yearnin' for tobacker and our dear fireside.

Swing 'er into stop-time, don't you let 'er droop!
(You're about as tuneful as a coyote with the croup!)
Ay, the cold wind bit when we drifted down the draw,
But we drifted on to comfort and to "Turkey in the Straw."

Snarlin' when the rain whipped, cussin' at the ford—
Ev'ry mile of twenty was a long discord,
But the night is brimmin' music and its glory is complete
When the eye is razzle-dazzled by the flip o' Shorty's feet!

Snappy for the dance, now, till she up and shoots!
(Don't he beat the devil's wife for jiggin' in 'is boots?)
Shorty got throwed high and we laughed till he was raw,
But tonight he's done forgot it prancin' "Turkey in the Straw."

Rainy dark or firelight, bacon rind or pie,
Livin' is a luxury that don't come high;
Oh, be happy and onruly while our years an luck allow,
For we all must die or marry less than forty years from now!

Lively on the last turn! lope 'er to the death!
(Reddy's soul is willin' but he's gettin' short o' breath.)
Ay, the storm wind sings and old trouble sucks his paw
When we have an hour of firelight set to "Turkey in the Straw."

The Outlaw

When my rope takes hold on a two-year-old,
    By the foot or the neck or the horn,
He kin plunge and fight till his eyes go white
    But I'll throw him as sure as you're born.
Though the taut ropes sing like a banjo string
    And the latigoes creak and strain,
Yet I got no fear of an outlaw steer
    And I'll tumble him on the plain.

    For a man is a man, but a steer is a beast,
        And the man is the boss of the herd,
    And each of the bunch, from the biggest to least,
        Must come down when he says the word.

When my leg swings 'cross on an outlaw hawse
    And my spurs clinch into his hide,
He kin r'ar and pitch over hill and ditch,
    But wherever he goes I'll ride.
Let 'im spin and flop like a crazy top
    Or flit like a wind-whipped smoke,
But he'll know the feel of my rowelled heel
    Till he's happy to own he's broke.

    For a man is a man and a hawse is a brute,
        And the hawse may be prince of his clan
    But he'll bow to the bit and the steel-shod boot
        And own that his boss is the man.

When the devil at rest underneath my vest
    Gets up and begins to paw
And my hot tongue strains at its bridle reins,
    Then I tackle the real outlaw.
When I get plumb riled and my sense goes wild
    And my temper is fractious growed,
If he'll hump his neck just a triflin' speck,
    Then it's dollars to dimes I'm throwed.

For a man is a man, but he's partly a beast.
He kin brag till he makes you deaf,
But the one lone brute, from the west to the east,
That he kaint quite break is himse'f.

The Tied Maverick

Lay on the iron! the tie holds fast
    And my wild record closes.
This maverick is down at last
    Just roped and tied with roses.
And one small girl's to blame for it,
Yet I don't fight with shame for it—
Lay on the iron; I'm game for it,
    Just roped and tied with roses.

I loped among the wildest band
    Of saddle-hatin' winners—
Gay colts that never felt a brand
    And scarred old outlaw sinners.
The wind was rein and guide to us;
The world was pasture wide to us
And our wild name was pride to us—
    High headed bronco sinners!

So, loose and light we raced and fought
    And every range we tasted,
But now, since I'm corralled and caught,
    I know them days were wasted.
From now, the all-day gait for me,
The trail that's hard but straight for me,
For down that trail, who'll wait for me!
    Ay! them old days were wasted!

But though I'm broke, I'll never be
    A saddle-marked old groaner,
For never worthless bronc like me
    Got such a gentle owner.
There could be colt days glad as mine
Or outlaw runs as mad as mine
Or rope-flung falls as bad as mine,
    But never such an owner.

Lay on the iron, and lay it red!
    I'll take it kind and clever.
Who wouldn't hold a prouder head
    To wear that mark forever?
I'll never break and stray from her;
I'd starve and die away from her.
Lay on the iron—it's play from her—
    And brand me hers forever!

Bachin'

Our lives are hid; our trails are strange;
    We're scattered through the West
In canyon cool, on blistered range
    Or windy mountain crest.
Wherever Nature drops her ears
    And bares her claws to scratch,
From Yuma to the north frontiers,
    You'll likely find the bach',
        You will,
    The shy and sober bach'!

Our days are sun and storm and mist,
    The same as any life,
Except that in our trouble list
    We never count a wife.
Each has a reason why he's lone,
    But keeps it 'neath his hat;
Or, if he's got to tell some one,
    Confides it to his cat,
        He does,
    Just tells it to his cat.

We're young or old or slow or fast,
    But all plumb versatyle.
The mighty bach' that fires the blast
    Kin serve up beans in style.
The bach' that ropes the plungin' cows
    Kin mix the biscuits true—
We earn our grub by drippin' brows
    And cook it by 'em too,
        We do,
    We cook it by 'em too.

We like to breathe unbranded air,
    Be free of foot and mind,
And go, or stay, or sing or swear,
    Whichever we're inclined.
An appetite, a conscience clear,
    A pipe that's rich and old
Are loves that always bless and cheer
    And never cry nor scold,
        They don't,
    They never cry nor scold.

Old Adam bached some ages back
    And smoked his pipe so free,
A-loafin' in a palm-leaf shack
    Beneath a mango tree.
He'd best have stuck to bachin' ways,
    And scripture proves the same,
For Adam's only happy days
    Was 'fore the woman came,
        They was,
    All 'fore the woman came.

The Song Of The Leather

When my trail stretches out to the edge of the sky
    Through the desert so empty and bright,
When I'm watchin' the miles as they go crawlin' by
    And a-hopin' I'll get there by night,
Then my hawse never speaks through the long sunny day,
    But my saddle he sings in his creaky old way:

      "Easy—easy—easy—
    For a temperit pace ain't a crime.
  Let your mount hit it steady, but give him his ease,
  For the sun hammers hard and there's never a breeze.
    We kin get there in plenty of time."

When I'm after some critter that's hit the high lope,
    And a-spurrin' my hawse till he flies,
When I'm watchin' the chances for throwin' my rope
    And a-winkin' the sweat from my eyes,
Then the leathers they squeal with the lunge and the swing
    And I work to the livelier tune that they sing:

      "Reach 'im! reach 'im! reach 'im!
    If you lather your hawse to the heel!
  There's a time to be slow and a time to be quick;
  Never mind if it's rough and the bushes are thick—
    Pull your hat down and fling in the steel!"

When I've rustled all day till I'm achin' for rest
    And I'm ordered a night-guard to ride,
With the tired little moon hangin' low in the west
    And my sleepiness fightin' my pride,
Then I nod and I blink at the dark herd below
    And the saddle he sings as my hawse paces slow:

      "Sleepy—sleepy—sleepy—
    We was ordered a close watch to keep,
  But I'll sing you a song in a drowsy old key;
  All the world is a-snoozin' so why shouldn't we?
    Go to sleep, pardner mine, go to sleep."

The Plainsmen

Men of the older, gentler soil,
    Loving the things that their fathers wrought—
Worn old fields of their fathers' toil,
    Scarred old hills where their fathers fought—
Loving their land for each ancient trace,
Like a mother dear for her wrinkled face,
      Such as they never can understand
      The way we have loved you, young, young land!

Born of a free, world-wandering race,
    Little we yearned o'er an oft-turned sod.
What did we care for the fathers' place,
    Having ours fresh from the hand of God?
Who feared the strangeness or wiles of you
When from the unreckoned miles of you,
      Thrilling the wind with a sweet command,
      Youth unto youth called, young, young land?

North, where the hurrying seasons changed
    Over great gray plains where the trails lay long,
Free as the sweeping Chinook we ranged,
    Setting our days to a saddle song.
Through the icy challenge you flung to us,
Through your shy Spring kisses that clung to us,
      Following far as the rainbow spanned,
      Fiercely we wooed you, young, young land!

South, where the sullen black mountains guard
    Limitless, shimmering lands of the sun,
Over blinding trails where the hoofs rang hard,
    Laughing or cursing, we rode and won.
Drunk with the virgin white fire of you,
Hotter than thirst was desire of you;
      Straight in our faces you burned your brand,
      Marking your chosen ones, young, young land.

When did we long for the sheltered gloom
    Of the older game with its cautious odds?
Gloried we always in sun and room,
    Spending our strength like the younger gods.
By the wild sweet ardor that ran in us,
By the pain that tested the man in us,
    By the shadowy springs and the glaring sand,
    You were our true-love, young, young land.

When the last free trail is a prim, fenced lane
    And our graves grow weeds through forgetful
      Mays,
Richer and statelier then you'll reign,
    Mother of men whom the world will praise.
And your sons will love you and sigh for you,
Labor and battle and die for you,
    But never the fondest will understand
    The way we have loved you, young, young land.

COLLECTED BY JOHN A. LOMAX

Whoopee Ti Yi Yo, Git Along Little Dogies

As I walked out one morning for pleasure,
I spied a cow-puncher all riding alone;
His hat was throwed back and his spurs was a jingling,
As he approached me a-singin' this song,

> Whoopee ti yi yo, git along little dogies,
> It's your misfortune, and none of my own.
> Whoopee ti yi yo, git along little dogies,
> For you know Wyoming will be your new home.

Early in the spring we round up the dogies,
Mark and brand and bob off their tails;
Round up our horses, load up the chuck-wagon,
Then throw the dogies upon the trail.

It's whooping and yelling and driving the dogies;
Oh how I wish you would go on;
It's whooping and punching and go on little dogies,
For you know Wyoming will be your new home.

Some boys goes up the trail for pleasure,
But that's where you get it most awfully wrong;
For you haven't any idea the trouble they give us
While we go driving them all along.

When the night comes on and we hold them on the
    bedground,
These little dogies that roll on so slow;
Roll up the herd and cut out the strays,
And roll the little dogies that never rolled before.

Your mother she was raised way down in Texas,
Where the jimson weed and sand-burrs grow;
Now we'll fill you up on prickly pear and cholla
Till you are ready for the trail to Idaho.

Oh, you'll be soup for Uncle Sam's Injuns;
"It's beef, heap beef," I hear them cry.
Git along, git along, git along little dogies
You're going to be beef steers by and by.

The Cowboy

All day long on the prairies I ride,
Not even a dog to trot by my side
My fire I kindle with chips gathered round,
My coffee I boil without being ground.

I wash in a pool and wipe on a sack;
I carry my wardrobe all on my back;
For want of an oven I cook bread in a pot,
And sleep on the ground for want of a cot.

My ceiling is the sky, my floor is the grass,
My music is the lowing of the herds as they pass;
My books are the brooks, my sermons the stones,
My parson is a wolf on his pulpit of bones.

And then if my cooking is not very complete
You can't blame me for wanting to eat.
But show me a man that sleeps more profound
Than the big puncher-boy who stretches himself on
     the ground.

My books teach me ever consistence to prize,
My sermons, that small things I should not despise;
My parson remarks from his pulpit of bones
That fortune favors those who look out for their own.

And then between me and love lies a gulf very wide.
Some lucky fellow may call her his bride.
My friends gently hint I am coming to grief,
But men must make money and women have beef.

But Cupid is always a friend to the bold,
And the best of his arrows are pointed with gold.
Society bans me so savage and dodge
That the Masons would ball me out of their lodge.

If I had hair on my chin, I might pass for the goat
That bore all the sins in the ages remote;
But why it is I can never understand,
For each of the patriarchs owned a big brand.

Abraham emigrated in search of a range,
And when water was scarce he wanted a change;
Old Isaac owned cattle in charge of Esau,
And Jacob punched cows for his father-in-law.

He started in business way down at bed rock,
And made quite a streak at handling stock;
Then David went from night-herding to using a sling;
And, winning the battle, he became a great king.
Then the shepherds, while herding the sheep on a hill,
Got a message from heaven of peace and goodwill.

A Home On The Range

Oh, give me a home where the buffalo roam,
Where the deer and the antelope play,
Where seldom is heard a discouraging word
And the skies are not cloudy all day.

   Home, home on the range,
   Where the deer and the antelope play;
   Where seldom is heard a discouraging word
   And the skies are not cloudy all day.

Where the air is so pure, the zephyrs so free,
The breezes so balmy and light,
That I would not exchange my home on the range
For all of the cities so bright.

The red man was pressed from this part of the West,
He's likely no more to return
To the banks of Red River where seldom if ever
Their flickering camp-fires burn.

How often at night when the heavens are bright
With the light from the glittering stars,
I stood here amazed and asked as I gazed
If their glory exceeds that of ours.

Oh, I love these wild flowers in this dear land of ours,
The curlew I love to hear scream,
And I love the white rocks and the antelope flocks
That graze on the mountain-tops green.

Oh, give me a land where the bright diamond sand
Flows leisurely down the stream;
Where the graceful white swan goes gliding along
Like a maid in a heavenly dream.

Then I would not exchange my home on the range,
Where the deer and the antelope play;
Where seldom is heard a discouraging word
And the skies are not cloudy all day.

Home, home on the range,
Where the deer and the antelope play;
Where seldom is heard a discouraging word
And the skies are not cloudy all day.

Texas Rangers

Come, all you Texas rangers, wherever you may be,
I'll tell you of some troubles that happened unto me.
My name is nothing extra, so it I will not tell,—
And here's to all you rangers, I am sure I wish you well.

It was at the age of sixteen that I joined the jolly band,
We marched from San Antonio down to the Rio Grande.
Our captain he informed us, perhaps he thought it right,
"Before we reach the station, boys, you'll surely have to fight."

And when the bugle sounded our captain gave command,
"To arms, to arms," he shouted, "and by your horses stand."
I saw the smoke ascending, it seemed to reach the sky;
The first thought that struck me, my time had come to die.

I saw the Indians coming, I heard them give the yell;
My feelings at that moment, no tongue can ever tell.
I saw the glittering lances, their arrows round me flew,
And all my strength it left me and all my courage too.

We fought full nine hours before the strife was o'er,
The like of dead and wounded I never saw before.
And when the sun was rising and the Indians they had fled,
We loaded up our rifles and counted up our dead.

And all of us were wounded, our noble captain slain,
And the sun was shining sadly across the bloody plain.
Sixteen as brave rangers as ever roamed the West,
Were buried by their comrades with arrows in their breast.

'Twas then I thought of mother, who to me in tears did say,
"To you they are all strangers, with me you had better stay."
I thought that she was childish, the best she did not know;
My mind was fixed on ranging and I was bound to go.

Perhaps you have a mother, likewise a sister too,
And maybe you have a sweetheart to weep and mourn for you;
If that be your situation, although you'd like to roam,
I'd advise you by experience, you had better stay at home.

I have seen the fruits of rambling, I know its hardships well;
I have crossed the Rocky Mountains, rode down the streets of
    hell;
I have been in the great Southwest where the wild Apaches roam,
And I tell you from experience you had better stay at home.

And now my song is ended; I guess I have sung enough;
The life of a ranger I am sure is very tough.
And here's to all you ladies, I am sure I wish you well,
I am bound to go a-ranging, so ladies, fare you well.

The Cowboy's Dream*

Last night as I lay on the prairie,
And looked at the stars in the sky,
I wondered if ever a cowboy
Would drift to that sweet by and by.

> Roll on, roll on;
> Roll on, little doggies, roll on, roll on,
> Roll on, roll on;
> Roll on, little dogies, roll on.

The road to that bright, happy region
Is a dim, narrow trail, so they say;
But the broad one that leads to perdition
Is posted and blazed all the way.

They say there will be a great round-up,
And cowboys, like dogies, will stand,
To be marked by the Riders of Judgment
Who are posted and know every brand.

I know there's many a stray cowboy
Who'll be lost at the great, final sale,
When he might have gone in the green pastures
Had he known of the dim, narrow trail.

I wonder if ever a cowboy
Stood ready for that Judgment Day,
And could say to the Boss of the Riders,
"I'm ready, come drive me away."

For they, like the cows that are locoed,
Stampede at the sight of a hand,
Are dragged with a rope to the round-up,
Or get marked with some crooked man's brand.

*Sung to the air of *My Bonnie Lies Over the Ocean.*

And I'm scared that I'll be a stray yearling,—
A maverick, unbranded on high,—
And get cut in the bunch with the "rusties"
When the Boss of the Riders goes by.

For they tell of another big owner
Whose ne'er overstocked, so they say,
But who always makes room for the sinner
Who drifts from the straight, narrow way.

They say he will never forget you,
That he knows every action and look;
So, for safety, you'd better get branded,
Have your name in the great Tally Book.

The Old Chisholm Trail

Come along, boys, and listen to my tale,
I'll tell you of my troubles on the old Chisholm trail.

    Coma ti yi youpy, youpy ya, youpy ya,
    Coma ti yi youpy, youpy ya.

I started up the trail October twenty-third,
I started up the trail with the 2-U herd.

Oh, a ten dollar hoss and a forty dollar saddle,—
And I'm goin' to punchin' Texas cattle.

I woke up one morning on the old Chisholm trail,
Rope in my hand and a cow by the tail.

I'm up in the mornin' afore daylight
And afore I sleep the moon shines bright.

Old Ben Bolt was a blamed good boss,
But he'd go to see the girls on a sore-backed hoss.

Old Ben Bolt was a fine old man
And you'd know there was whiskey wherever he'd land.

My hoss throwed me off at the creek called Mud,
My hoss throwed me off round the 2-U herd.

Last time I saw him he was going cross the level
A-kicking up his heels and a-running like the devil.

It's cloudy in the West, a-looking like rain,
And my damned old slicker's in the wagon again.

Crippled my hoss, I don't know how,
Ropin' at the horns of a 2-U cow.

We hit Caldwell and we hit her on the fly,
We bedded down the cattle on the hill close by.

No chaps, no slicker, and it's pouring down rain,
And I swear, by god, I'll never night-herd again.

Feet in the stirrups, and seat in the saddle,
I hung and rattled with them long-horn cattle.

Last night I was on guard and the leader broke the
    ranks,
I hit my horse down the shoulders and I spurred him in
    the flanks.

The wind commenced to blow, and the rain began to
    fall,
Hit looked, by grab, like we was goin' to loss 'em all.

I jumped in the saddle and grabbed holt the horn,
Best blamed cow-puncher ever was born.

I popped my foot in the stirrup and gave a little yell,
The tail cattle broke and the leaders went to hell.

I don't give a damn if they never do stop;
I'll ride as long as an eight-day clock.

Foot in the stirrup and hand on the horn,
Best damned cowboy ever was born.

I herded and I hollered and I done very well,
Till the boss said, "Boys, just let 'em go to hell."

Stray in the herd and the boss said kill it,
So I shot him in the rump with the handle of the
    skillet.

We rounded 'em up and put 'em on the cars,
And that was the last of the old Two Bars.

Oh it's bacon and beans most every day,—
I'd as soon be a-eatin' prairie hay.

I'm on my best horse and I'm goin' at a run,
I'm the quickest shootin' cowboy that ever pulled a
  gun.

I went to the wagon to get my roll,
To come back to Texas, dad-burn my soul.

I went to the boss to draw my roll,
He had it figgered out I was nine dollars in the hole.

I'll sell my outfit just as soon as can,
I won't punch cattle for no damned man.

Goin' back to town to draw my money,
Goin' back home to see my honey.

With my knees in the saddle and my seat in the sky,
I'll quit punching cows in the sweet by and by.

  Coma ti yi youpy, youpy ya, youpy ya,
  Coma ti yi youpy, youpy ya.

Dogie Song

The cow-bosses are good-hearted chunks,
Some short, some heavy, more long;
But don't matter what he looks like,
They all sing the same old song.
On the plains, in the mountains, in the valleys,
In the south where the days are long,
The bosses are different fellows;
Still they sing the same old song.

> "Sift along, don't ride so slow;
> Haven't got much time but a long round to go.
> Quirt him in the shoulders and rake him down the
>   hip;
> I've cut you toppy mounts, boys, now pair off and
>   rip.
> Bunch the herd at the old meet,
> Then beat 'em on the tail;
> Whip 'em up and down the sides
> And hit the shortest trail."

Jesse James

Jesse James was a lad that killed a–many a man;
He robbed the Danville train.
But that dirty little coward that shot Mr. Howard
Has laid poor Jesse in his grave.

>   Poor Jesse had a wife to mourn for his life,
>   Three children, they were brave.
>   But that dirty little, coward that shot Mr. Howard
>   Has laid poor Jesse in his grave.

It was Robert Ford, that dirty little coward,
I wonder how he does feel,
For he ate of Jesse's bread and he slept in Jesse's bed,
Then laid poor Jesse in his grave.

Jesse was a man, a friend to the poor,
He never would see a man suffer pain;
And with his brother Frank he robbed the Chicago
    bank,
And stopped the Glendale train.

It was his brother Frank that robbed the Gallatin bank,
And carried the money from the town;
It was in this very place that they had a little race,
For they shot Captain Sheets to the ground.

They went to the crossing not very far from there,
And there they did the same;
With the agent on his knees, he delivered up the keys
To the outlaws, Frank and Jesse James.

It was on Wednesday night, the moon was shining
    bright,
They robbed the Glendale train;
The people they did say, for many miles away,
It was robbed by Frank and Jesse James.

It was on Saturday night, Jesse was at home
Talking with his family brave,
Robert Ford came along like a thief in the night
And laid poor Jesse in his grave.

The people held their breath when they heard of Jesse's
    death,
And wondered how he ever came to die.
It was one of the gang called little Robert Ford,
He shot poor Jesse on the sly.

Jesse went to his rest with his hand on his breast;
The devil will be upon his knee.
He was born one day in the county of Clay
And came from a solitary race.

This song was made by Billy Gashade,
As soon as the news did arrive;
He said there was no man with the law in his hand
Who could take Jesse James when alive.

Mustang Gray

There once was a noble ranger,
They called him Mustang Gray;
He left his home when but a youth,
Went ranging far away.

But he'll go no more a-ranging,
The savage to affright;
He has heard his last war-whoop,
And fought his last fight.

He ne'er would sleep within a tent,
No comforts would he know;
But like a brave old Tex-i-an,
A-ranging he would go.

When Texas was invaded
By a mighty tyrant foe,
He mounted his noble war-horse
And a-ranging he did go.

Once he was taken prisoner,
Bound in chains upon the way,
He wore the yoke of bondage
Through the streets of Monterey.

A senorita loved him,
And followed by his side;
She opened the gates and gave to him
Her father's steed to ride.

God bless the senorita,
The belle of Monterey,
She opened wide the prison door
And let him ride away.

And when this veteran's life was spent,
It was his last command
To bury him on Texas soil
On the banks of the Rio Grande;

And there the lonely traveler,
When passing by his grave,
Will shed a farewell tear
O'er the bravest of the brave.

> And he'll go no more a-ranging,
> The savage to affright;
> He has heard his last war-whoop,
> And fought his last fight.

The Cowboy's Lament

As I walked out in the streets of Laredo,
As I walked out in Laredo one day,
I spied a poor cowboy wrapped up in white linen,
Wrapped up in white linen as cold as the clay.

> "Oh, beat the drum slowly and play the fife lowly,
> Play the Dead March as you carry me along;
> Take me to the green valley, there lay the sod o'er me,
> For I'm a young cowboy and I know I've done wrong.

"I see by your outfit that you are a cowboy,"
These words he did say as I boldly stepped by.
Come sit down beside me and hear my sad story;
I was shot in the breast and I know I must die.

> "Let sixteen gamblers come handle my coffin,
> Let sixteen cowboys come sing me a song,
> Take me to the graveyard and lay the sod o'er me,
> For I'm a poor cowboy and I know I've done wrong.

"My friends and relations, they live in the Nation,
They know not where their boy has gone.
He first came to Texas and hired to a ranchman,
Oh, I'm a young cowboy and I know I've done wrong.

"Go write a letter to my gray-haired mother,
And carry the same to my sister so dear;
But not a word of this shall you mention
When a crowd gathers round you my story to hear.

> "Then beat your drum lowly, and play your fife slowly,
> Beat the Dead March as you carry me along;
> We all love our cowboys so young and so handsome,
> We all love our cowboys although they've done wrong.

"There is another more dear than a sister,
She'll bitterly weep when she hears I am gone.
There is another who will win her affections,
For I'm a young cowboy and they say I've done wrong.

"Go gather around you a crowd of young cowboys,
And tell them the story of this my sad fate;
Tell one and the other before they go further
To stop their wild roving before 'tis too late.

"Oh, muffle your drums, then play your fifes merrily;
Play the Dead March as you go along.
And fire your guns right over my coffin;
There goes an unfortunate boy to his home

"It was once in the saddle I used to go dashing,
It was once in the saddle I used to go gay;
First to the dram-house, then to the card-house,
Got shot in the breast, I am dying to-day.

"Get six jolly cowboys to carry my coffin;
Get six pretty maidens to bear up my pall.
Put bunches of roses all over my coffin,
Put roses to deaden the clods as they fall.

"Then swing your rope slowly and rattle your spurs lowly,
And give a wild whoop as you carry me along;
And in the grave throw me and roll the sod o'er me,
For I'm a young cowboy and I know I've done wrong.

"Go bring me a cup, a cup of cold water,
To cool my parched lips," the cowboy said;
Before I turned, the spirit had left him
And gone to its Giver,—the cowboy was dead.

We beat the drum slowly and played the fife lowly,
And bitterly wept as we bore him along;
For we all loved our comrade, so brave, young, and handsome,
We all loved our comrade although he'd done wrong.

Bill Peters, The Stage Driver

Bill Peters was a hustler
From Independence town;
He warn't a college scholar
Nor man of great renown,
But Bill had a way o' doing things
And doin' 'em up brown.

Bill driv the stage from Independence
Up to the Smokey Hill;
And everybody knowed him thar
As Independence Bill,—
Thar warn't no feller on the route
That driv with half the skill.

Bill driv four pair of horses,
Same as you'd drive a team,
And you'd think you was a-travelin'
On a railroad driv by steam;
And he'd git thar on time, you bet,
Or Bill 'u'd bust a seam.

He carried mail and passengers,
And he started on the dot,
And them teams o' his'n, so they say,
Was never known to trot;
But they went it in a gallop
And kept their axles hot.

When Bill's stage 'u'd bust a tire,
Or something 'u'd break down,
He'd hustle round and patch her up
And start off with a bound;
And the wheels o' that old shack o' his
Scarce ever touched the ground.

And Bill didn't low no foolin',
And when Inguns hove in sight
And bullets rattled at the stage,
He druv with all his might;
He'd holler, "Fellers, give 'em hell,
I ain't got time to fight."

Then the way them wheels 'u'd rattle,
And the way the dust 'u'd fly,
You'd think a million cattle,
Had stampeded and gone by;
But the mail 'u'd get thar just the same,
If the horses had to die.

He driv that stage for many a year
Along the Smokey Hill,
And a pile o' wild Comanches
Did Bill Peters have to kill,—
And I reckon if he'd had good luck
He'd been a drivin' still.

But he chanced one day to run agin
A bullet made o' lead,
Which was harder than he bargained for
And now poor Bill is dead;
And when they brung his body home
A barrel of tears was shed.

Drinking Song

Drink that rot gut, drink that rot gut,
Drink that red eye, boys;
It don't make a damn wherever we land,
We hit her up for joy.

We've lived in the saddle and ridden trail,
Drink old Jordan, boys,
We'll go whooping and yelling, we'll all go a-helling;
Drink her to our joy.

Whoop-ee! drink that rot gut, drink that red nose,
Whenever you get to town;
Drink it straight and swig it mighty,
Till the world goes round and round!

The Trail To Mexico

I made up my mind to change my way
And quit my crowd that was so gay,
To leave my native home for a while
And to travel west for many a mile.

Whoo-a-whoo-a-whoo-a-whoo.

'Twas all in the merry month of May
When I started for Texas far away,
I left my darling girl behind,—
She said her heart was only mine.

Whoo-a-whoo-a-whoo-a-whoo.

Oh, it was when I embraced her in my arms
I thought she had ten thousand charms;
Her caresses were soft, her kisses were sweet,
Saying, "We will get married next time we meet."

Whoo-a-whoo-a-whoo-a-whoo.

It was in the year of eighty-three
That A.J. Stinson hired me.
He says, "Young fellow, I want you to go
And drive this herd to Mexico."

Whoo-a-whoo-a-whoo-a-whoo.

The first horse they gave me was an old black
With two big set-fasts on his back;
I padded him with gunny-sacks and my bedding all;
He went up, then down, and I got a fall.

Whoo-a-whoo-a-whoo-a-whoo.

The next they gave me was an old gray,
I'll remember him till my dying day.
And if I had to swear to the fact,
I believe he was worse off than the black.

Whoo-a-whoo-a-whoo-a-whoo.

Oh, it was early in the year
When I went on trail to drive the steer.
I stood my guard through sleet and snow
While on the trail to Mexico.

Whoo-a-whoo-a-whoo-a-whoo.

Oh, it was a long and lonesome go
As our herd rolled on to Mexico;
With laughter light and the cowboy's song
To Mexico we rolled along.

Whoo-a-whoo-a-whoo-a-whoo.

When I arrived in Mexico
I wanted to see my love but could not go;
So I wrote a letter, a letter to my dear,
But not a word from her could I hear.

Whoo-a-whoo-a-whoo-a-whoo.

When I arrived at the once loved home
I called for the darling of my own;
They said she had married a richer life,
Therefore, wild cowboy, seek another wife.

Whoo-a-whoo-a-whoo-a-whoo.

Oh, the girl she is married I do adore,
And I cannot stay at home any more;
I'll cut my way to a foreign land
Or I'll go back west to my cowboy band.

Whoo-a-whoo-a-whoo-a-whoo.

I'll go back to the Western land,
I'll hunt up my old cowboy band,—
Where the girls are few and the boys are true
And a false-hearted love I never knew.

Whoo-a-whoo-a-whoo-a-whoo.

"O Buddie, O Buddie, please stay at home,
Don't be forever on the roam.
There is many a girl more true than I,
So pray don't go where the bullets fly."

Whoo-a-whoo-a-whoo-a-whoo.

It's curse your gold and your silver too,
God pity a girl that won't prove true;
I'll travel West where the bullets fly,
I'll stay on the trail till the day I die."

Whoo-a-whoo-a-whoo-a-whoo.

Bucking Broncho

My love is a rider, wild bronchos he breaks,
Though he's promised to quit it, just for my sake.
He ties up one foot, the saddle puts on,
With a swing and a jump he is mounted and gone.

The first time I met him, 'twas early one spring,
Riding a broncho, a high-headed thing.
He tipped me a wink as he gaily did go;
For he wished me to look at his bucking broncho.

The next time I saw him 'twas late in the fall,
Swinging the girls at Tomlinson's ball.
He laughed and he talked as we danced to and fro,
Promised never to ride on another broncho.

He made me some presents, among them a ring;
The return that I made him was a far better thing;
'Twas a young maiden's heart, I'd have you all know;
He's won it by riding his bucking broncho.

My love has a gun, and that gun he can use,
But he's quit his gun fighting as well as his booze;
And he's sold him his saddle, his spurs, and his rope,
And there's no more cow punching, and that's what I
    hope.

My love has a gun that has gone to the bad,
Which makes poor old Jimmy feel pretty damn sad;
For the gun it shoots high and the gun it shoots low,
And it wobbles about like a bucking broncho.

Now all you young maidens, where'er you reside,
Beware of the cowboy who swings the raw-hide;
He'll court you and pet you and leave you and go
In the spring up the trail on his bucking broncho.

The Dying Cowboy

"O bury me not on the lone prairie,"
These words came low and mournfully
From the pallid lips of a youth who lay
On his dying bed at the close of day.

He had wailed in pain till o'er his brow
Death's shadows fast were gathering now;
He thought of his home and his loved ones nigh
As the cowboys gathered to see him die.

   "O bury me not on the lone prairie
   Where the wild cayotes will howl o'er me,
   In a narrow grave just six by three,
   O bury me not on the lone prairie.

"In fancy I listen to the well known words
Of the free, wild winds and the song of the birds;
I think of home and the cottage in the bower
And the scenes I loved in my childhood's hour.

"It matters not, I've oft been told,
Where the body lies when the heart grows cold;
Yet grant, Oh grant this wish to me,
O bury me not on the lone prairie.

   "O then bury me not on the lone prairie,
   In a narrow grave six foot by three,
   Where the buffalo paws o'er a prairie sea,
   O bury me not on the lone prairie.

"I've always wished to be laid when I died
In the little churchyard on the green hillside;
By my father's grave, there let mine be,
And bury me on the lone prairie

"Let my death slumber be where my mother's prayer
And a sister's tear will mingle there,
Where my friends can come and weep o'er me;
O bury me not on the lone prairie.

"O bury me not on the lone prairie
In a narrow grave just six by three,
Where the buzzard waits and the wind blows free;
Then bury me not on the lone prairie.

"There is another whose tears may be shed
For one who lies on a prairie bed;
It pained me then and it pains me now;—
She has curled these locks, she has kissed this brow.

"These locks she has curled, shall the rattlesnake kiss?
This brow she has kissed, shall the cold grave press?
For the sake of the loved ones that will weep for me
O bury me not on the lone prairie.

"O bury me not on the lone prairie
Where the wild cayotes will howl o'er me,
Where the buzzard beats and the wind goes free,
O bury me not on the lone prairie.

"O bury my not," and his voice failed there,
But we took no heed to his dying prayer;
In a narrow grave just six by three
We buried him there on the lone prairie.

Where the dew-drops glow and the butterflies rest,
And the flower's bloom o'er the prairies crest;
Where the wild cayote and winds sport free
On a wet saddle blanket lay a cowboy-ee.

"O bury me not on the lone prairie
Where the wild cayotes will howl o'er me,
Where the rattlesnakes hiss and the crow flies free
O bury me not on the lone prairie."

O we buried him there on the lone prairie
Where the wild rose blooms and the wind blows free,
O his pale young face nevermore to see,—
For we buried him there on the lone prairie.

Yes, we buried him there on the lone prairie
Where the owl all night hoots mournfully,
And the blizzard beats and the winds blow free
O'er his lowly grave on the lone prairie.

And the cowboys now as they roam the plain,—
For they marked the spot where his bones were lain,—
Fling a handful of roses o'er his grave,
With a prayer to Him who his soul will save.

"O bury me not on the lone prairie
Where the wolves can howl and growl o'er me;
Fling a handful of roses o'er my grave
With a prayer to Him who my soul will save.

Sam Bass

Sam Bass was born in Indiana, it was his native home,
And at the age of seventeen young Sam began to roam.
Sam first came out to Texas a cowboy for to be,—
A kinder-hearted fellow you seldom ever see.

Sam use'd to deal in race stock, one called the Denton mare,
He matched her in scrub races, and took her to the Fair.
Sam used to coin the money and spent it just as free,
He always drank good whiskey wherever he might be.

Sam left the Collin's ranch in the merry month of May
With a herd of Texas cattle the Black Hills for to see,
Sold out in Custer City and then got on a spree,—
A harder set of cowboys you seldom ever see.

On their way back to Texas they robbed the U. P. train,
And then split up in couples and started out again.
Joe Collins and his partner were overtaken soon,
With all their hard-earned money they had to meet their doom.

Sam made it back to Texas all right side up with care;
Rode into the town of Denton with all his friends to share.
Sam's life was short in Texas; three robberies did he do,
He robbed all the passenger mail, and express cars too.

Sam had four companions—four bold and daring lads—
They were Richardson, Jackson, Joe Collins, and Old Dad;
Four more bold and daring cowboys the rangers never knew,
They whipped the Texas rangers and ran the boys in blue.

Sam had another companion, called Arkansas for short,
Was shot by a Texas ranger by the name of Thomas Floyd;
Oh, Tom is a big six-footer and thinks he's mighty fly,
But I can tell you his racket,—he's a deadbeat on the sly.

Jim Murphy was arrested, and then released on bail;
He jumped his bond at Tyler and then took the train for Terrell;
But Mayor Jones had posted Jim and that was all a stall,
'Twas only a plan to capture Sam before the coming fall.

Sam met his fate at Round Rock, July the twenty-first,
They pierced poor Sam with rifle balls and emptied out his purse.
Poor Sam he is a corpse and six foot under clay,
And Jackson's in the bushes trying to get away.

Jim had borrowed Sam's good gold and didn't want to pay,
The only shot he saw was to give poor Sam away.
He sold out Sam and Barnes and left their friends to mourn,—
Oh, what a scorching Jim will get when Gabriel blows his horn.

And so he sold out Sam and Barnes and left their friends to
     mourn,
Oh, what a scorching Jim will get when Gabriel blows his horn.
Perhaps he's got to heaven, there's none of us can say,
But if I'm right in my surmise he's gone the other way.

The Pecos Queen

Where the Pecos River winds and turns in its journey to the sea,
From its white walls of sand and rock striving ever to be free,
Near the highest railroad bridge that all these modern times have
    seen,
Dwells fair young Patty Morehead, the Pecos River queen.

She is known by every cowboy on the Pecos River wide,
They know full well that she can shoot, that she can rope and
    ride.
She goes to every round-up, every cow work without fail,
Looking out for her cattle, branded "walking hog on rail."

She made her start in cattle, yes, made it with her rope;
Can tie down every maverick before it can strike a lope.
She can rope and tie and brand it as quick as any man;
She's voted by all cowboys an A-I top cow hand.

Across the Comstock railroad bridge, the highest in the West,
Patty rode her horse one day, a lover's heart to test;
For he told her he would gladly risk all dangers for her sake—
But the puncher wouldn't follow, so she's still without a mate.

Little Joe, The Wrangler

It's little Joe, the wrangler, he'll wrangle never more,
His days with the *remuda* they are o'er;
'Twas a year ago last April when he rode into our camp,—
Just a little Texas stray and all alone,—
On a little Texas pony he called "Chaw."
With his brogan shoes and overalls, a tougher kid
You never in your life before had saw.

His saddle was a Texas "kak," built many years ago,
With an O. K. spur on one foot lightly swung;
His "hot roll" in a cotton sack so loosely tied behind,
And his canteen from his saddle-horn was swung.
He said that he had to leave his home, his pa had married twice;
And his new ma whipped him every day or two;
So he saddled up old Chaw one night and lit a shuck this way,
And he's now trying to paddle his own canoe.

He said if we would give him work, he'd do the best he could,
Though he didn't know straight up about a cow;
So the boss he cut him out a mount and kindly put him on,
For he sorta liked this little kid somehow.
Learned him to wrangle horses and to try to know them all,
And get them in at daylight if he could;
To follow the chuck-wagon and always hitch the team,
And to help the *cocinero* rustle wood.

We had driven to the Pecos, the weather being fine;
We had camped on the south side in a bend;
When a norther commenced blowin', we had doubled up our
    guard,
For it taken all of us to hold them in.
Little Joe, the wrangler, was called out with the rest;
Though the kid had scarcely reached the herd,
When the cattle they stampeded, like a hailstorm long they fled,
Then we were all a-ridin' for the lead.

'Midst the streaks of lightin' a horse we could see in the lead,
'Twas Little Joe, the wrangler, in the lead;
He was riding Old Blue Rocket with a slicker o'er his head,
A tryin' to check the cattle in their speed.
At last we got them milling and kinda quieted down,
And the extra guard back to the wagon went;
But there was one a-missin' and we knew it at a glance,
'Twas our little Texas stray, poor Wrangling Joe.

The next morning just at day break, we found where Rocket fell,
Down in a washout twenty feet below;
And beneath the horse, mashed to a pulp,—his spur had rung the
    knell,—
Was our little Texas stray, poor Wrangling Joe.

The Jolly Cowboy

My lover, he is a cowboy, he's brave and kind and true,
He rides a Spanish pony, he throws a lasso, too;
And when he comes to see me our vows we do redeem,
He throws his arms around me and thus begins to sing:

"Ho, I'm a jolly cowboy, from Texas now I hail,
Give me my quirt and pony, I'm ready for the trail;
I love the rolling prairies, they're free from care and strife,
Behind a herd of longhorns I'll journey all my life.

"When early dawn is breaking and we are far away,
We fall into our saddles, we round-up all the day;
We rope, we brand, we ear-mark, I tell you we are smart,
And when the herd is ready, for Kansas then we start.

"Oh, I am a Texas cowboy, lighthearted, brave, and free,
To roam the wide, wide prairie, 'tis always joy to me.
My trusty little pony is my companion true,
O'er creeks and hills and rivers he's sure to pull me through.

"When threatening clouds do gather and herded lightnings flash,
And heavy rain drops splatter, and rolling thunders crash;
What keeps the herd from running, stampeding far and wide?
The cowboy's long, low whistle and singing by their side.

"When in Kansas City, our boss he pays us up,
We loaf around the city and take a parting cup;
We bid farewell to city life, from noisy crowds we come,
And back to dear old Texas, the cowboy's native home."

"Oh, he is coming back to marry the only girl he loves,
He says I am his darling, I am his own true love;
Some day we two will marry and then no more he'll roam,
But settle down with Mary in a cozy little home.

"Ho, I'm a jolly cowboy, from Texas now I hail,
Give me my bond to Mary, I'll quit the Lone Star trail.
I love the rolling prairies, they're free from care and strife,
But I'll quit the herd of longhorns for the sake of my little
    wife."

Jack O' Diamonds

O Mollie, O Mollie, it is for your sake alone
That I leave my old parents, my house and my home,
That I leave my old parents, you caused me to roam,—
I am a rabble soldier and Dixie is my home.

    Jack o' diamonds, Jack o' diamonds,
    I know you of old,
    You've robbed my poor pockets
    Of silver and gold.
    Whiskey, you villain,
    You've been my downfall,
    You've kicked me, you've cuffed me,
    But I love you for all.

My foot's in my stirrup, my bridle's in my hand,
I'm going to leave sweet Mollie, the fairest in the land.
Her parents don't like me, they say I'm too poor,
They say I'm unworthy to enter her door.

They say I drink whiskey; my money is my own,
And them that don't like me can leave me alone.
I'll eat when I'm hungry, I'll drink when I'm dry,
And when I get thirsty I'll lay down and cry.

    It's beefsteak when I'm hungry,
    And whiskey when I'm dry,
    Greenbacks when I'm hard up,
    And heaven when I die.
    Rye whiskey, rye whiskey,
    Rye whiskey, I cry,
    If I don't get rye whiskey,
    I surely will die.
        O Baby, O Baby, I've told you before,
        Do make me a pallet, I'll lie on the floor.

I will build me a big castle on yonder mountain high,
Where my true love can see me when she comes riding
    by,
Where my true love can see me and help me to
    mourn,—
I am a rabble soldier and Dixie is my home.

I'll get up in my saddle, my quirt I'll take in hand,
I'll think of you, Mollie, when in some far distant land,
I'll think of you, Mollie, you caused me to roam,—
I am a rabble soldier and Dixie is my home.

    If the ocean was whiskey,
    And I was a duck,
    I'd dive to the bottom
    To get one sweet sup;
    But the ocean ain't whiskey,
    And I ain't a duck,
    So I'll play Jack o' diamonds
    And then we'll get drunk.
        O Baby, O Baby, I've told you before,
        Do make me a pallet, I'll lie on the floor.

I've rambled and trambled this wide world around,
But it's for the rabble army, dear Mollie, I'm bound,
It is to the rabble army, dear Mollie, I roam,—
I am a rabble soldier and Dixie is my home.

I have rambled and gambled all my money away,
But it's with the rabble army, O Mollie, I must stay,
It is with the rabble army, O Mollie I must roam,—
I am a rabble soldier and Dixie is my home.

Jack o' diamonds, Jack o' diamonds,
I know you of old,
You've robbed my poor pockets
Of silver and gold.
Rye whiskey, rye whiskey,
Rye whiskey I cry,
If you don't give me rye whiskey
I'll lie down and die.
    O Baby, O Baby, I've told you, before,
    Do make me a pallet, I'll lie on the floor.

Night-Herding Song

(by Harry Stephens)

Oh, slow up, dogies, quit your roving round,
You have wandered and tramped all over the ground;
Oh, graze along, dogies, and feed kinda slow,
And don't forever be on the go,—
Oh, move slow, dogies, move slow.

Hi-oo, hi-oo, oo-oo.

I have circle-herded, trail-herded, night-herded, and
    cross-herded, too,
But to keep you together, that's what I can't do;
My horse is leg weary and I'm awful tired,
But if I let you get away I'm sure to get fired,—
Bunch up, little dogies, bunch up.

Hi-oo, hi-oo, oo-oo.

O say, little dogies, when you goin' to lay down
And quit this forever siftin' around?
My limbs are weary, my seat is sore;
Oh, lay down, dogies, like you've laid before,—
Lay down, little dogies, lay down.

Hi-oo, hi-oo, oo-oo.

Oh, lay still, dogies, since you have laid down,
Stretch away out on the big open ground;
Snore loud, little dogies, and drown the wild sound
That will all go away when the day rolls round,—
Lay still, little dogies, lay still.

Hi-oo, hi-oo, oo-oo.

Utah Carroll

And as, my friend, you ask me what makes me sad and still,
And why my brow is darkened like the clouds upon the hill;
Run in your pony closer and I'll tell to you the tale
Of Utah Carroll, my partner, and his last ride on the trail.

'Mid the cactus and the thistles of Mexico's fair lands,
Where the cattle roam in thousands, a-many a herd and brand,
There is a grave with neither headstone, neither date nor name,—
There lies my partner sleeping in the land from which I came.

We rode the range together and had rode it side by side;
I loved him as a brother, I wept when Utah died;
We were rounding up one morning, our work was almost done,
When on the side the cattle started on a mad and fearless run.

The boss man's little daughter was holding on that side.
She rushed; the cattle saw the blanket, they charged with
    maddened fear.
And little Varro, seeing the danger, turned her pony a pace
And leaning in the saddle, tied the blanket in its place.

In leaning, she lost her balance and fell in front of that wild tide.
Utah's voice controlled the round-up. "Lay still, little Varro," he
    cried.
His only hope was to raise her, to catch her at full speed,
And oft-times he had been known to catch the trail rope off his
    steed.

His pony reached the maiden with a firm and steady bound;
Utah swung out from the saddle to catch her from the ground.
He swung out from the saddle, I thought her safe from harm,
As he swung in his saddle to raise her in his arm.

But the cinches of his saddle had not been felt before,
And his back cinch snapt asunder and he fell by the side of Varro.
He picked up the blanket and swung it over his head
And started across the prairie; "Lay still, little Varro," he said.

Well, he got the stampede turned and saved little Varro, his friend.
Then he turned to face the cattle and meet his fatal end.
His six-shooter from his pocket, from the scabbard he quickly
    drew,—
He was bound to die defended as all young cowboys do.

His six-shooter flashed like lightning, the report rang loud and
    clear;
As the cattle rushed in and killed him he dropped the leading
    steer.
And when we broke the circle where Utah's body lay,
With many a wound and bruise his young life ebbed away.

"And in some future morning," I heard the preacher say,
"I hope we'll all meet Utah at the round-up far away."
Then we wrapped him in a blanket sent by his little friend,
And it was that very red blanket that brought him to his end.

A Cow Camp On The Range

Oh, the prairie dogs are screaming,
And the birds are on the wing,
See the heel fly chase the heifer, boys!
'Tis the first class sign of spring.
The elm wood is budding,
The earth is turning green.
See the pretty things of nature
That make life a pleasant dream!

I'm just living through the winter
To enjoy the coming change,
For there is no place so homelike
As a cow camp on the range.
The boss is smiling radiant,
Radiant as the setting sun;
For he knows he's stealing glories,
For he ain't a-cussin' none.

The cook is at the chuck-box
Whistling "Heifers in the Green,"
Making baking powder biscuits, boys,
While the pot is biling beans.
The boys untie their bedding
And unroll it on the run,
For they are in a monstrous hurry
For the supper's almost done.

"Here's your bloody wolf bait,"
Cried the cook's familiar voice
As he climbed the wagon wheel
To watch the cowboys all rejoice.
Then all thoughts were turned from reverence
To a plate of beef and beans,
As we graze on beef and biscuits
Like yearlings on the range.

To the dickens with your city
Where they herd the brainless brats,
On a range so badly crowded
There ain't room to cuss the cat.
This life is not so sumptuous,
I'm not longing for a change,
For there is no place so homelike
As a cow camp on the range.

The Cowboy's Life

(Attributed to James Barton Adams)

The bawl of a steer,
To a cowboy's ear,
Is music of sweetest strain;
And the yelping notes
Of the gray cayotes
To him are a glad refrain.

And his jolly songs
Speed him along,
As he thinks of the little gal
With golden hair
Who is waiting there
At the bars of the home corral.

For a kingly crown
In the noisy town
His saddle he wouldn't change;
No life so free
As the life we see
Way out on the Yaso range.

His eyes are bright
And his heart as light
As the smoke of his cigarette;
There's never a care
For his soul to bear,
No trouble to make him fret,

The rapid beat
Of his broncho's feet
On the sod as he speeds along,
Keeps living time
To the ringing rhyme
Of his rollicking cowboy song.

Hike it, cowboys,
For the range away
On the back of a bronc of steel,
With a careless flirt
Of the raw-hide quirt
And a dig of a roweled heel!

The winds may blow
And the thunder growl
Or the breezes may safely moan;—
A cowboy's life
Is a royal life,
His saddle his kingly throne.

Saddle up, boys,
For the work is play
When love's in the cowboy's eyes,—
When his heart is light
As the clouds of white
That swim in the summer skies.

New National Anthem

My country, 'tis of thee,
Land where things used to be
So cheap, we croak.
Land of the mavericks,
Land of the puncher's tricks,
Thy culture-inroad pricks
The hide of this peeler-bloke.

Some of the punchers swear
That what they eat and wear
Takes all their calves.
Others vow that they
Eat only once a day
Jerked beef and prairie hay
Washed down with tallow salves.

These salty-dogs** but crave
To pull them out the grave
just one Kiowa spur.
They know they still will dine
On flesh and beef the time;
But give us, Lord divine,
One "hen-fruit stir."*

Our father's land, with thee,
Best trails of liberty,
We chose to stop.
We don't exactly like
So soon to henceward hike,
But hell, we'll take the pike
If this don't stop.

** Cowboy Dude
* Pancake

Bibliography

Brininstool, E.A. *Trail Dust of a Maverick*. New York: Dodd, Mead and Company, 1914.

Carr, Robert V. *Cowboy Lyrics*. Chicago: W.B. Conkey Company, 1908.

_____. *Black Hills Ballads*. Denver: The Reed Publishing Company, 1902.

Chapman, Arthur. *Out Where the West Begins*. Boston and New York: Houghton Mifflin Company, 1917.

Chittenden, William Lawrence. *Ranch Verses*. New York: G.P. Putnam's Sons: 1893.

Clark, Charles Badger Jr. *Sun and Saddle Leather*. Boston: The Gorham Press, 1917.

Griggs, Nathan Kirk. *Lyrics of the Lariat*. Chicago: Fleming H. Revell Company, 1893.

Lomax, John A., ed. *Cowboy Songs and Other Frontier Ballads*. New York: Sturgis & Walter Company, 1916.